Printed in the United States of America.

First Printing, August 2025

ISBN: 979-8-9994492-0-7

Man In The Arena LLC
200 SW 30th Avenue
Cape Coral, FL 33991
www.mybasketballarena.com

BASKETBALL PROGRAM PLAYBOOK *for* PLAYERS

2025-2026

NAME: _____

TEAM: _____

COACH: _____

LEVEL: VARSITY   JV   FRESHMAN

GRADE: 9TH   10TH   11TH   12TH

ABOUT MAN IN THE ARENA, LLC

MYBASKETBALLARENA.COM

Man In The Arena exists to help improve basketball coaches, players, and teams. While there are almost unlimited resources available to improve skill, technique, and overall Basketball IQ, there are few resources designed to help organize a holistic approach to growing a team's ability to win and conquer the mental game behind basketball. We focus not on the Xs and Os, but the mental grit, toughness, and tenacity that every team needs to succeed. With these strategies, we focus on the easy-to-implement tools that both coaches and players can adopt to drive the kind of team culture that is required to win.

Every basketball coach in America has undoubtedly asked their players this question at one time or another: "Who wants to win more? Us or them?" Our approach changes the basic nature of that question: "What will we do that is different than anyone else, in order to win?" The answer to that question is and should be different for each team. Our work exists not to prescribe specific plays or drills, but to provide the structure by which you can answer that important question for your team. This work supports both coaches and players as they take their game to the next level.

To that end, we are inspired and motivated by this now-famous quote from President Theodore Roosevelt's "Man In The Arena" speech, which also serves as the inspiration for the name of this company. This quote informs how we build the tools any team needs, the methodologies we create, and the approach we organize for long-term team success.

"It is not the critic who counts; not the man who points out how the strong man stumbles, or where the doer of deeds could have done them better. The credit belongs to the man who is actually in the arena, whose face is marred by dust and sweat and blood; who strives valiantly; who errs, who comes short again and again, because there is no effort without error and shortcoming; but who does actually strive to do the deeds; who knows the great enthusiasms, the great devotions; who spends himself in a worthy cause; who at the best knows in the end the triumph of high achievement, and who at the worst, if he fails, at least fails while daring greatly, so that his place shall never be with those cold and timid souls who neither know victory nor defeat."

- Theodore Roosevelt, 1910

TABLE OF CONTENTS

PURPOSE OF THIS BOOK

The "Basketball Program Playbook for Players" is a tool for players who want to take their game and their team beyond the Xs and Os of basketball. Throughout this book you will find easy-to-adopt tools that you and your team can use. These tools are designed to help prepare you for practices, games, and increasing your Basketball IQ, while ensuring you and your coach are on the same page.

This book will not teach you drills, plays, or sets that you and your team should use (that's the role of your coach). Instead, this book is designed to support your efforts in becoming a better basketball player, buying in to a common team goal, and better understanding your role. Between school and practice, we know that players often lack the time to go above and beyond what is required in practice and for games. This book helps YOU organize your efforts, develop mental grit, and focus on the strategies that will help you improve your overall game.

To be a successful basketball player, you must manage competing priorities:

- Taking care of business in the classroom is always your first priority, if you want to continue playing basketball.
- Growing your physical endurance and strength is a never-ending requirement.
- Skill development for your role will help you compete for spots on your team and during games.
- Building your Basketball IQ will set you apart from other players once you truly KNOW the game of basketball.
- Being a leader within your team (and school) makes you a valuable asset in the eyes of any coach.
- Knowing how to be coachable, not just from your coaches, ensures you are constantly improving.
- Managing your relationships with family and friends gives you balance while also ensuring you maintain your responsibilities away from basketball.

This is a long list of priorities, but these expectations are very real for today's basketball players, especially if you want to play in college. This can become an overwhelming feeling for many players. It's not enough to just want to be a great player. Instead, great players need the tools and organization to compete and manage these priorities. This book is designed to help you do just that, and is built based on three core concepts that are written throughout this book.

What follows is an introduction to these three concepts. In the "Buying In" section of this

book, we'll go into greater detail, but continue reading on as you prepare to use this book for your season.

DARE GREATLY - with inspiration from the quote found earlier in this book, the Dare Greatly concept focuses on the team itself, negating the impact of critics and naysayers outside of the program (including fans and opponents, alike). This concept focuses not on winning, but developing the grit necessary to win (despite the critics). Thinking logically, our actions in any activity always lead to the results; in this instance, our efforts, discipline, and organization lead to grit, tenacity, and perseverance. Those results then lead to the outcome. If done right, the outcome is a win, on and off the court.

I DO, WE DO, YOU DO - too often, we forget that the basketball court is in fact a classroom. While most players will say the court is more fun and engaging than a classroom, we can use this approach to build your Basketball IQ. With this method, the "I Do" part is lead by the coach, teaching skill development, conditioning, and different sets; the "We Do" is the heart of practice, where players practice what has been taught; the "You Do" is often left to game-time only, but that can be a mistake. By empowering you and your teammates to become teachers/leaders yourselves on and off the court, you will better develop the skills that increase your IQ, beyond the Xs and Os.

THE 1% APPROACH - to make these concepts real, players need to understand how to best organize the approach to growth. The 1% Approach is a simple math question: from day one of the season, can you improve 1% day by day? This approach makes growth more manageable and matches your physical effort, during practice for example, with a required mental commitment. It allows for open and honest (and often-times vulnerable) discussions with coaches about where, how, and why you need to improve; and most importantly, it puts within reach the concept of growth for you, especially if you struggle with the mental game of basketball.

There is no single solution that will solve every problem or challenge you face as a player. However, the tools in this book have been designed and tested to increase your skills on and off the court with strategies that create a winning culture. The organized approach to these tools that are found in this book will allow you, and your team, to tackle the hurdles that all teams face.

We wish you luck!

HOW TO USE THIS BOOK AS A PLAYER

This book is broken down in five major sections, plus some additional resources at the end. Review these sections first before you dive into the book.

SECTION 1: BUYING IN

In this section, you'll explore the three components that help you understand how to approach this book, and your basketball season as well. These sections are important to understand and you should consider completing these sections with teammates, coaches, or as a program (based on your coach's directions).

- First, you'll dive deep into the "Dare Greatly" concept. This helps teach you about conquering the mental game of basketball, understanding the value of tenacity and grit, and applying these ideas to your own basketball program.
- Then, you'll learn about the "I Do, We Do, You Do" approach to learning and growing throughout the season. If you ever get bored at a practice, wonder what else you can do to grow outside of practice, or want to become a better leader for your team, this approach will help you understand a greater role you have in your growth.
- And finally, you'll develop three primary goals to accomplish this season using The 1% Approach. You'll develop a clear and targeted set of goals that you can manage throughout the season (and beyond).

SECTION 2: PROGRAM PLAYS

In this section, you'll write out and draw the different plays that your team uses in a game. Lead by your coaching staff, this is your opportunity to not just memorize the plays on the court, but truly learn about the plays, why you use them, what kind of teams to use these plays against, and what your specific role in the play is. As you complete each of these plays within this book, the goal is that you become an expert on this play to the point that you can teach it to others if you had to.

SECTION 3: WEEKLY PLANNING

In this section, you will organize your efforts off the court that make you an all-around better player. Week by week, you'll list your schedule of practices and games, describe the actions you will take that week for each of your three 1% goals, and manage your practice, game, and school preparation through a weekly checklist.

It's important that you, as a player, fully buy in to the weekly planning process. This is an opportunity for you to develop habits that help you become a better player and teammate. By making this a habit, your off court preparation becomes a true asset for you on the court.

SECTION 4: FILM & SCOUTING REPORTS

In this section, you'll compete film and/ or scouting reports throughout the season. This section helps you prepare for games, but more importantly helps you increase your Basketball IQ. While it's easy to be a passive viewer of film, this section helps you become an active and engaged analyst of games, recognizing plays, strengths, weaknesses, and trends of teams.

This section also helps you become a leader within your team. As you become more confident with film and scouting analysis, you can use those skills during practice and in games for real-time use. Ask any coach, including yours, about the value of a leader who has strong Basketball IQ and you'll see right away why you might want to increase these skills.

SECTION 5: POST-GAME REVIEW

In this section, you'll review each of your games throughout the season. You will analyze both your and your team's efforts during the game, and identify areas to improve for the next game. This section connects the Basketball IQ you are building with analysis for your actual games throughout the season.

ADDITIONAL RESOURCES

At the end of this book (beginning on page 160), you'll find example forms filled out for each of these sections to help you complete this book, blank court diagrams to fill in as you need, and a section for additional notes.

Buying In

BUYING IN

This book is designed to help you, as a player, better prepare for, manage, and succeed during your basketball season. This book is NOT designed to teach you the Xs and Os of basketball (that is the job of your coach and other resources); instead, this book will help you develop the habits, routines, and skills necessary to achieve excellence on AND off the court.

You may have heard the saying "extraordinary people do extra-ordinary things". You may have also heard your coach ask you or your team "What are you willing to do different that your competitors won't?" For most players, the answers to that question focus on the things you do on the court, during a practice, or in a game. For elite players, at any age, the answers to that question must go beyond your physical effort. Being extraordinary will require any athlete to commit physically AND mentally.

By now, this information is likely not new to you. However, you may still be curious about what physical and mental commitment truly looks like. Most players step onto a basketball court and want to be the very best they can be, leading to a win or a championship. While everyone wants to be successful, not all players actually know what to do to reach that goal. In fact, the things that extraordinary players do that ordinary players do not usually isn't very clear. This book helps give you the tools to be able to make your desired goal a reality, and become extraordinary.

To do this, you must buy in. This requires two commitments:
- First, you must buy in to your coach's program. He or she knows the game, understands what it takes to win, and juggles the different types of talent on the team to create the winning plays that lead to success. Every program is different, as it should be. But as a teammate, it is your duty and responsibility to buy in to your coach's program. When players buy in as a team, wins follow.
- And second, you must buy in to the work YOU must do to become the best player you can be. This includes the work you do during practice and games, of course. However, this also includes the mental commitment you make, and the work you do as a result.

In this section, and throughout this book, you will develop the tools to buy in to the work you are responsible for, on and off the court. Let's explore the three major components of the buy in process in the following pages. Once you do that, you'll know how to approach the rest of this book and become an extraordinary player.

DARE GREATLY

Let's take a deeper dive into the quote found earlier in this book, often referred to as the "Man In The Arena" speech by President Theodore Roosevelt. While this is a historical reference, don't get too bored too fast. This quote can help you transform how you approach the game of basketball, and how you develop the grit you need when times get tough.

First, let's explore the quote line by line. We've added some extra thoughts on each line to help you think deeper about the meaning.

QUOTE: LINE-BY-LINE	THOUGHTS & QUESTIONS
"It is not the critic who counts; not the man who points out how the strong man stumbles, or where the doer of deeds could have done them better.	Who are the critics in the game of basketball? How do they show up? What kinds of things do they do as a critic?
The credit belongs to the man who is actually in the arena, whose face is marred by dust and sweat and blood; who strives valiantly; who errs, who comes short again and again,	Think of the arena as the basketball court. Think about the times your face has been marred, when you have made great effort, even when you make a mistake.
because there is no effort without error and shortcoming; but who does actually strive to do the deeds;	Our efforts will always lead to, sometimes, error. But can we pick ourselves up time after time after error?
who knows the great enthusiasms, the great devotions; who spends himself in a worthy cause;	Think about the joys and thrills of your efforts, of your common goals as a team.
who at the best knows in the end the triumph of high achievement, and who at the worst, if he fails, at least fails while daring greatly,	When you win, the feeling is triumphant. But, if you lose at least you do so in great effort so that critics no longer matter.
so that his place shall never be with those cold and timid souls who neither know victory nor defeat."	If we dare greatly, win or lose, we will know both victory and defeat, but our efforts can't be described as timid or cold.

On the next page, let's explore what it means to dare greatly, for you.

WHAT DOES IT MEAN TO YOU TO DARE GREATLY?

Think about the quote you read on the previous page and respond to the following questions. You can do this individually, in groups, or as a team depending on your coach's directions:

QUESTION	RESPONSE
Who are the critics that show up in your world of basketball? By definition, are they in the arena with us?	
Are there critics that we should listen to, even if they mean well? Why or why not?	
For you, what does it mean to be in the "arena"? What actions that you take represent you being in the arena?	
If you dare greatly in your efforts, why does it make winning or losing better than just winning without daring greatly?	
Have the critics (no matter who they are) ever impacted how you have practiced or played? If so, describe.	
To dare greatly means we can grow from our efforts, even if we win or lose. Why?	
Based on this quote, what should we focus on more: winning or daring greatly? Why?	

Now, think of the following question from a very personal perspective. Based on what you know today, what are 3 things YOU should focus on to dare greatly?

1.	2.	3.

I DO, WE DO, YOU DO

Here's a secret that not all coaches will reveal: the basketball court is just another classroom. When we think of a classroom, we don't usually think of a gym or court, but the best coaches know that to teach basketball, and to grow Basketball IQ, we should think of the court as a classroom. Why?

By now, you probably have a good sense of how you learn things. Some people are **visual learners**, where seeing things helps them grow knowledge. Some people are **auditory learners**, learning best by hearing something in order to comprehend it. And still, others are **kinesthetic learners**, where they require hands-on activities and physical engagement. However you learn, the same is true on the basketball court.

Coaches teach their teams using different approaches as well. One of the best ways to learn, no matter your style, is to become part of the teaching method known as "I Do, We Do, You Do". Why is this part of the buy in process for growing yourself in basketball? Because this approach requires YOU to take an active role and responsibility in your growth.

Let's look at the approach:

I DO - this is where your coach will model a play, a skill, or a strategy to you during practice. Generally speaking, if your coach is talking through a drill or introducing a new topic, this is the I Do phase.

WE DO - this is the phase where, in practice, you and your teammates are working on the court with your coach. Sometimes this may be done in "slow motion" before running it live.

YOU DO - in this phase, you and your teammates take responsibility and fully lead the skill, drill, or play. This can be done in practice, but we most often see it in a game. The coach is on the sideline and you as a player are fully responsible.

But, perhaps there are other opportunities for learning. Can you as a player take more responsibility, especially in the "You Do" phase? We think the answer to that is yes.

Throughout this book, we will help you take more responsibility for the learning process in the "You Do" phase, especially through learning your program's plays, managing your weekly planning, completing film and scouting reports, and conducting post-game reviews. All of these steps will help you increase your Basketball IQ, and become more active in your growth, especially off the court.

THE 1% APPROACH

So far, you've thought about two important concepts that will help you build your skills, talent, and grit as a basketball player: (1) the importance of daring greatly, and (2) the importance of taking a more active and responsible role in learning/growing.

Now, we will help make those concepts real with The 1% Approach.

Think about a goal you have for improving your game, like becoming a better rebounder, for example. At the start of the season, your skills in rebounding are referred to as the "baseline"; the baseline is your starting point. With The 1% Approach, we think about improving from your baseline throughout the season.

In this example, let's say you will have 60 practices throughout the season. Based on those practices, could we create a goal that says you will improve your rebounding skills by just 1% each practice? Let's look at the math:

Baseline: **6 rebounds per game, on average**
After 17 practices: **7 rebounds per game = +1 possession**
After 34 practices: **8 rebounds per game = +2 possessions**
After 50 practices: **9 rebounds per game = +3 possessions**

In less than 1 season, you have increased your rebounding rate by 50%, adding on average a potential 3 more possessions per game. How many games have you played in your career where 3 more possessions would have made the difference between a win or a loss? Imagine if a few of your teammates had this same goal; now we're talking about a significant increase in winning plays.

The 1% Approach is simple math that helps you approach mentally tough goals. Tackle your big goals 1% at a time and the challenge becomes a lot easier to manage. From day to day, practice to practice, or game to game, you may not notice a big change, but you have now organized your brain around the essential steps you must do to actually improve. When growth feels slow, we can get down on ourselves. When we have a blueprint for our growth, we stay the course.

Your 1% goals can be focused on anything that will help you improve your game, including both on and off the court strategies. You should also talk with your coach and your teammates about these goals and come to agreement on what makes most sense for you AND your team. Ideas for goals can include: shooting, rebounding, steals, speed, endurance, team leadership, film analysis, nutrition, strength training, school/practice attendance, team engagement, and many more areas.

Below, identify 3 goals that you will strive for using The 1% Approach. Describe in detail and identify how you will measure growth (can be stats, coach input, and teammate input, among other things). Then, track your progress throughout the season.

THE 1% APPROACH

GROWTH AREA #1
DESCRIBE GOAL:

HOW WILL GROWTH BE MEASURED?

TRACK PROGRESS:

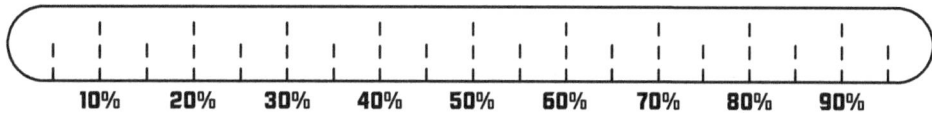

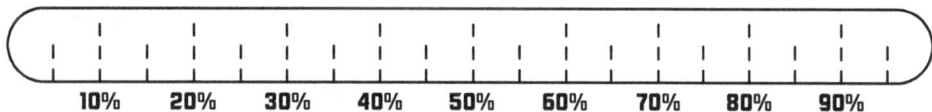

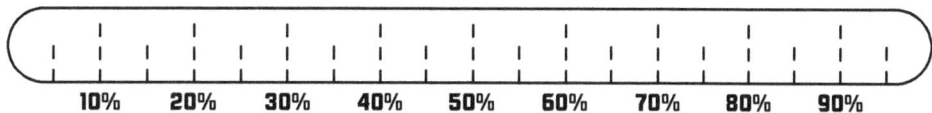

10%　20%　30%　40%　50%　60%　70%　80%　90%

GROWTH AREA #2
DESCRIBE GOAL:

HOW WILL GROWTH BE MEASURED?

TRACK PROGRESS:

10%　20%　30%　40%　50%　60%　70%　80%　90%

GROWTH AREA #3
DESCRIBE GOAL:

HOW WILL GROWTH BE MEASURED?

TRACK PROGRESS:

10%　20%　30%　40%　50%　60%　70%　80%　90%

NOTES ON BUYING IN

_____

_____

_____

_____

_____

_____

_____

_____

_____

_____

_____

_____

_____

_____

_____

_____

_____

_____

_____

_____

_____

_____

NOTES ON BUYING IN

NOTES ON BUYING IN

Program Plays

PROGRAM PLAYS

In the following pages, you will write out and draw the plays your program uses, both offensively and defensively.

As you write these plays, think about the "big picture" for each of these plays:
- When should this play be used?
- Why is this play effective?
- What type of team do we use this play against?

In addition, think about your specific role in the play:
- What do I do in this play?
- Why do I do this?
- How do my actions impact the rest of my team on the court?

Below, list the plays that your team uses as you learn them and fill out this section. This will serve as your quick guide to the plays and the page it is located on.

OFFENSIVE PLAYS		DEFENSIVE PLAYS	
NAME OF PLAY	PAGE #	NAME OF PLAY	PAGE #

NAME OF PLAY:

TYPE:

        OFFENSIVE   **DEFENSIVE**

IN WORDS, DESCRIBE THIS PLAY:

WHEN SHOULD THIS PLAY BE USED?

WHY IS THIS PLAY EFFECTIVE?

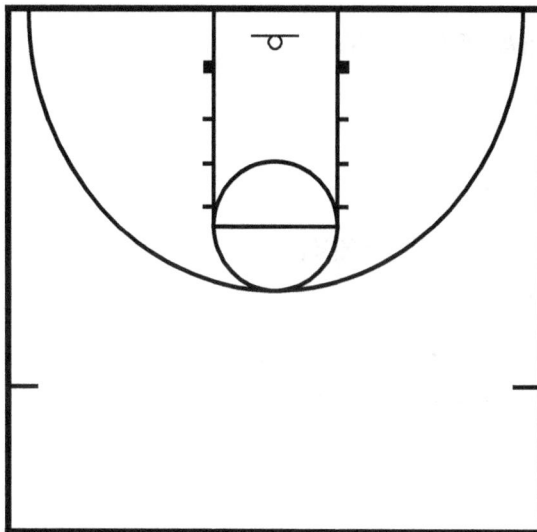

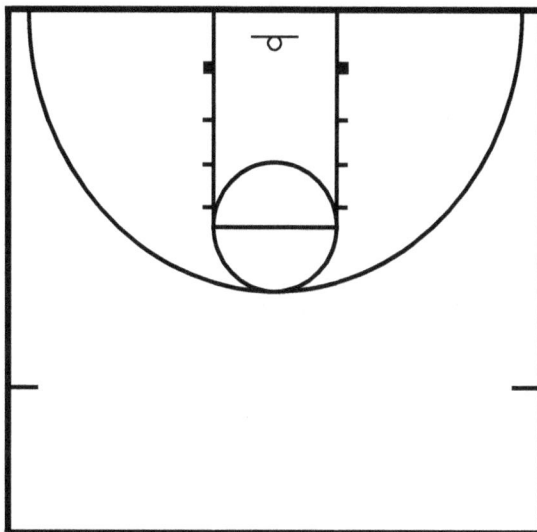

WHAT IS MY ROLE IN THIS PLAY?

WHAT KIND OF TEAM DO WE USE THIS PLAY AGAINST?

NAME OF PLAY:

- -

TYPE:

        OFFENSIVE   **DEFENSIVE**

IN WORDS, DESCRIBE THIS PLAY:

- -

WHEN SHOULD THIS PLAY BE USED?

WHAT IS MY ROLE IN THIS PLAY?

- -

WHY IS THIS PLAY EFFECTIVE?

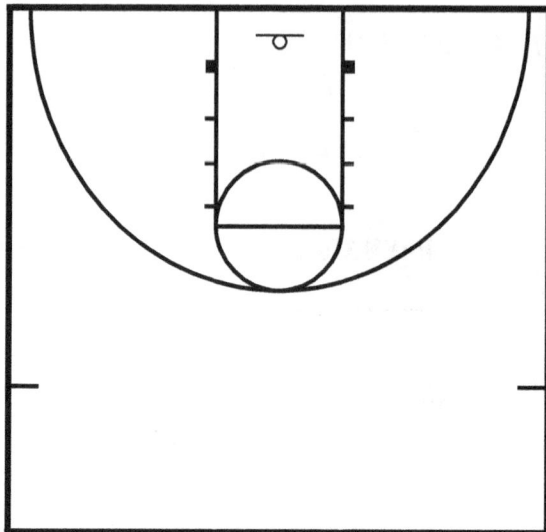

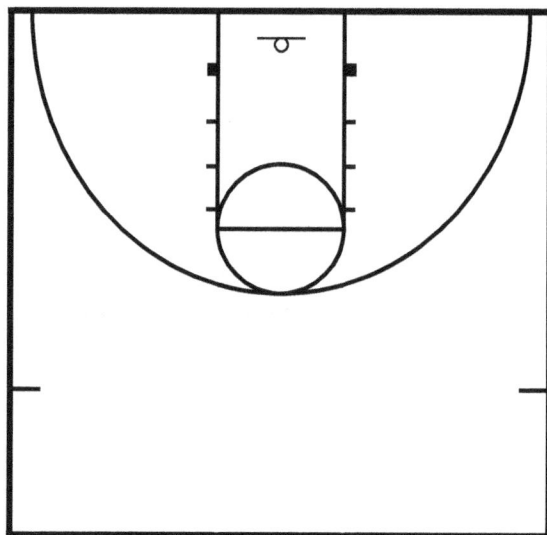

- -

WHAT KIND OF TEAM DO WE USE THIS PLAY AGAINST?

NAME OF PLAY:

TYPE:

      OFFENSIVE   **DEFENSIVE**

IN WORDS, DESCRIBE THIS PLAY:

WHEN SHOULD THIS PLAY BE USED?

WHY IS THIS PLAY EFFECTIVE?

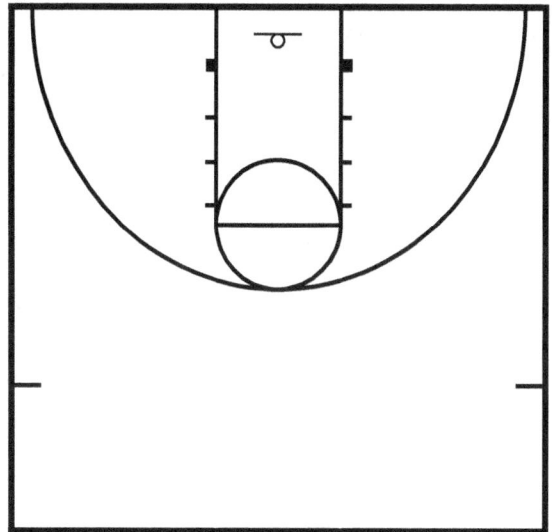

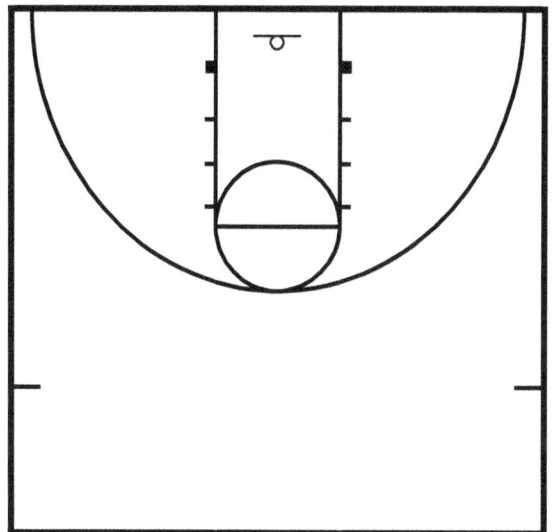

WHAT IS MY ROLE IN THIS PLAY?

WHAT KIND OF TEAM DO WE USE THIS PLAY AGAINST?

NAME OF PLAY:

TYPE:

OFFENSIVE   **DEFENSIVE**

IN WORDS, DESCRIBE THIS PLAY:

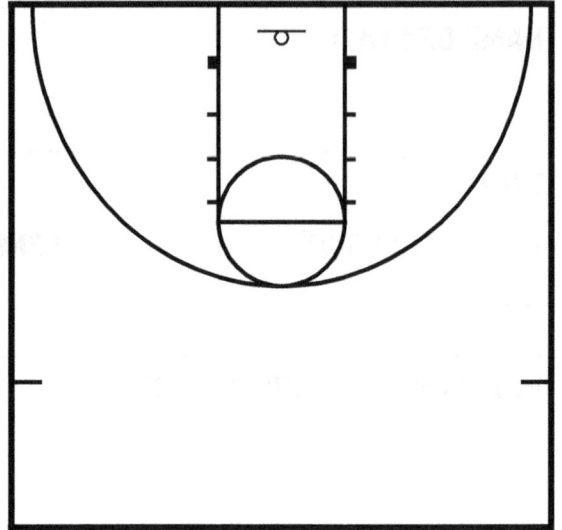

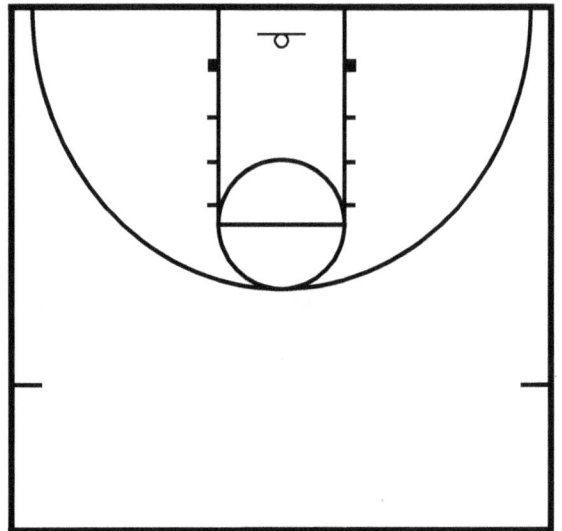

WHEN SHOULD THIS PLAY BE USED?

WHY IS THIS PLAY EFFECTIVE?

WHAT IS MY ROLE IN THIS PLAY?

WHAT KIND OF TEAM DO WE USE THIS PLAY AGAINST?

NAME OF PLAY:

TYPE:

OFFENSIVE   **DEFENSIVE**

IN WORDS, DESCRIBE THIS PLAY:

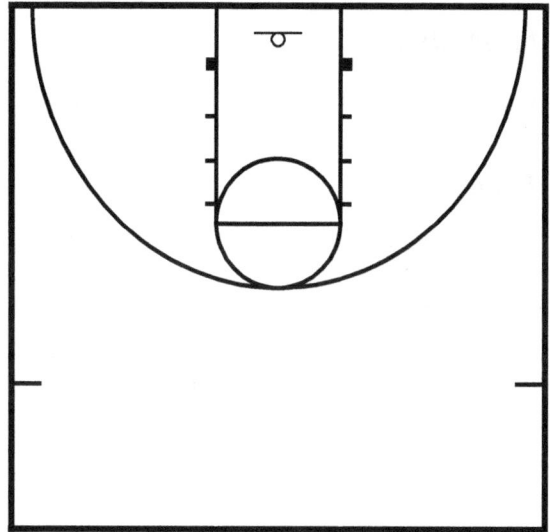

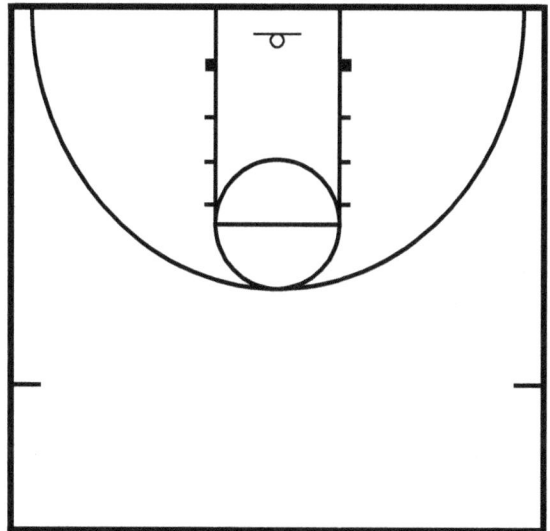

WHEN SHOULD THIS PLAY BE USED?

WHY IS THIS PLAY EFFECTIVE?

WHAT IS MY ROLE IN THIS PLAY?

WHAT KIND OF TEAM DO WE USE THIS PLAY AGAINST?

NAME OF PLAY:

TYPE:

      OFFENSIVE   DEFENSIVE

IN WORDS, DESCRIBE THIS PLAY:

WHEN SHOULD THIS PLAY BE USED?

WHY IS THIS PLAY EFFECTIVE?

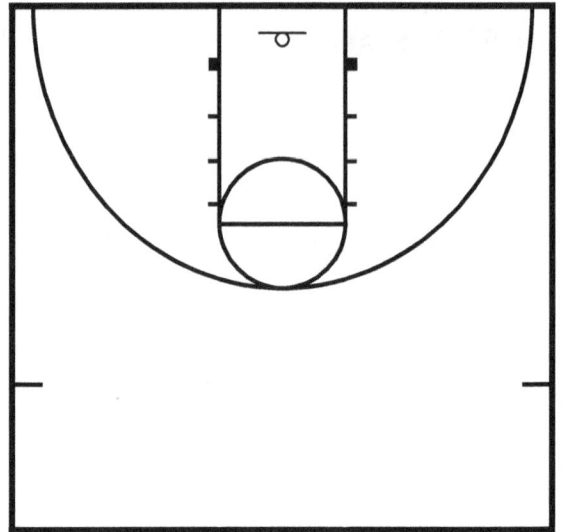

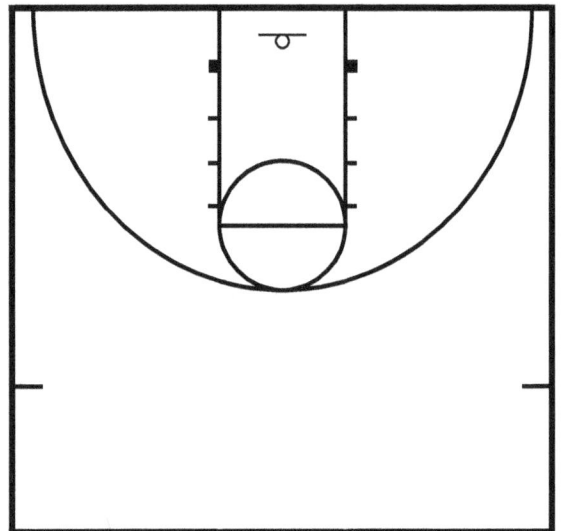

WHAT IS MY ROLE IN THIS PLAY?

WHAT KIND OF TEAM DO WE USE THIS PLAY AGAINST?

NAME OF PLAY:

TYPE:

OFFENSIVE   **DEFENSIVE**

IN WORDS, DESCRIBE THIS PLAY:

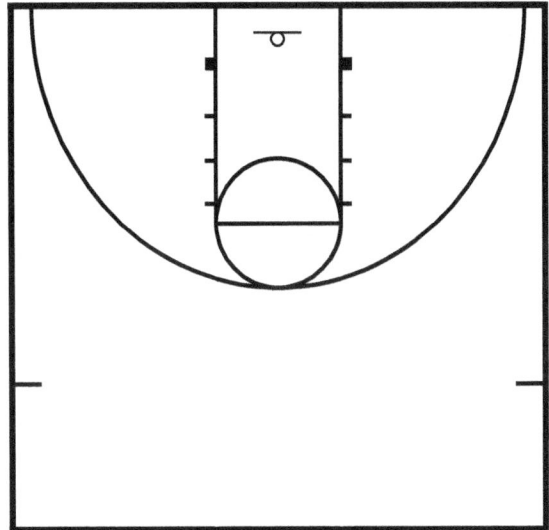

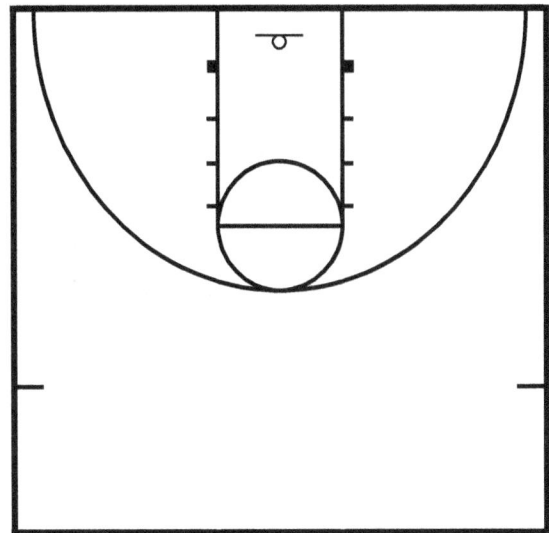

WHEN SHOULD THIS PLAY BE USED?

WHY IS THIS PLAY EFFECTIVE?

WHAT IS MY ROLE IN THIS PLAY?

WHAT KIND OF TEAM DO WE USE THIS PLAY AGAINST?

NAME OF PLAY:

TYPE:

      OFFENSIVE   **DEFENSIVE**

IN WORDS, DESCRIBE THIS PLAY:

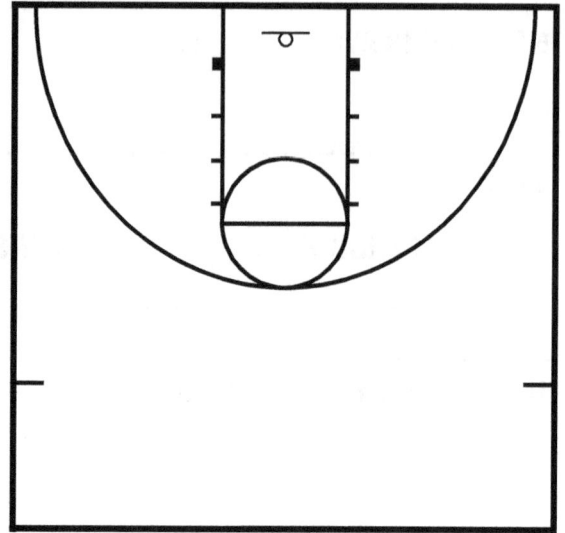

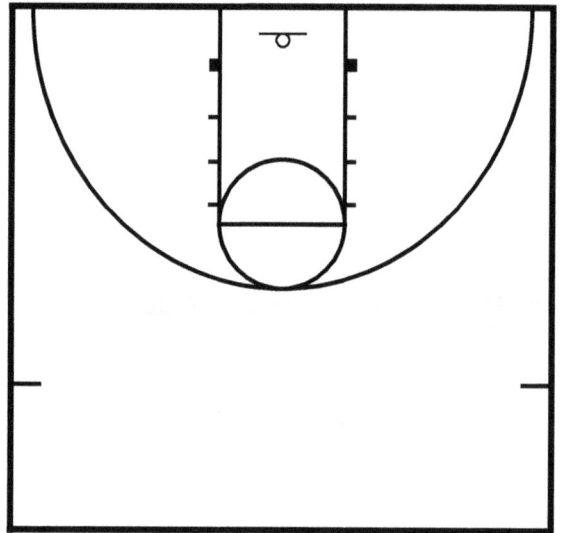

WHEN SHOULD THIS PLAY BE USED?

WHY IS THIS PLAY EFFECTIVE?

WHAT IS MY ROLE IN THIS PLAY?

WHAT KIND OF TEAM DO WE USE THIS PLAY AGAINST?

NAME OF PLAY:

TYPE:

OFFENSIVE   **DEFENSIVE**

IN WORDS, DESCRIBE THIS PLAY:

WHEN SHOULD THIS PLAY BE USED?

WHY IS THIS PLAY EFFECTIVE?

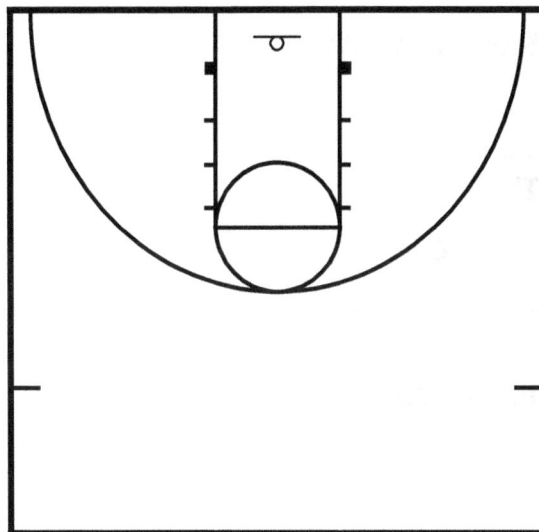

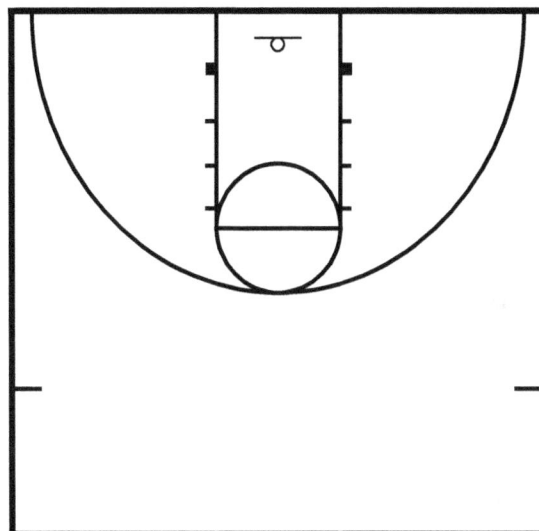

WHAT IS MY ROLE IN THIS PLAY?

WHAT KIND OF TEAM DO WE USE THIS PLAY AGAINST?

NAME OF PLAY:

TYPE:

OFFENSIVE   **DEFENSIVE**

IN WORDS, DESCRIBE THIS PLAY:

WHEN SHOULD THIS PLAY BE USED?

WHY IS THIS PLAY EFFECTIVE?

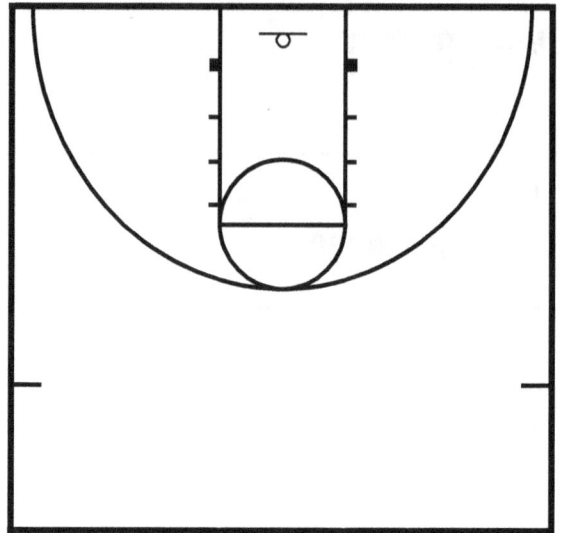

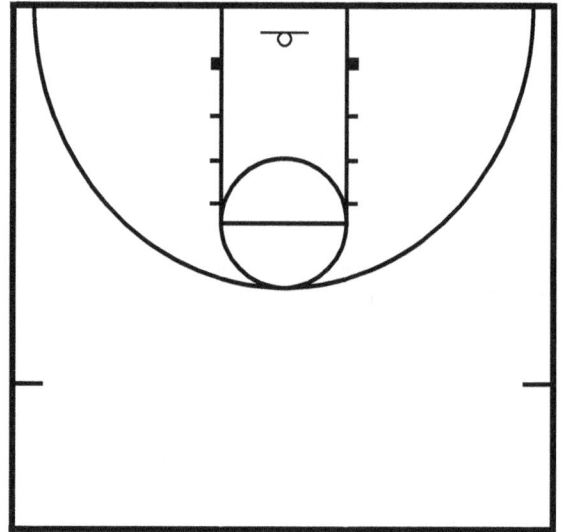

WHAT IS MY ROLE IN THIS PLAY?

WHAT KIND OF TEAM DO WE USE THIS PLAY AGAINST?

NAME OF PLAY:

TYPE:

OFFENSIVE   **DEFENSIVE**

IN WORDS, DESCRIBE THIS PLAY:

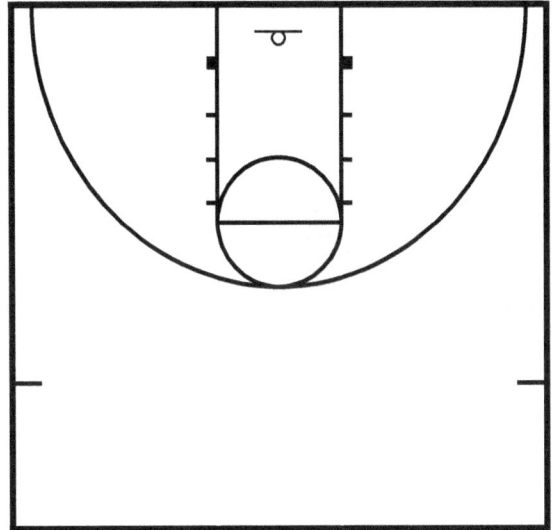

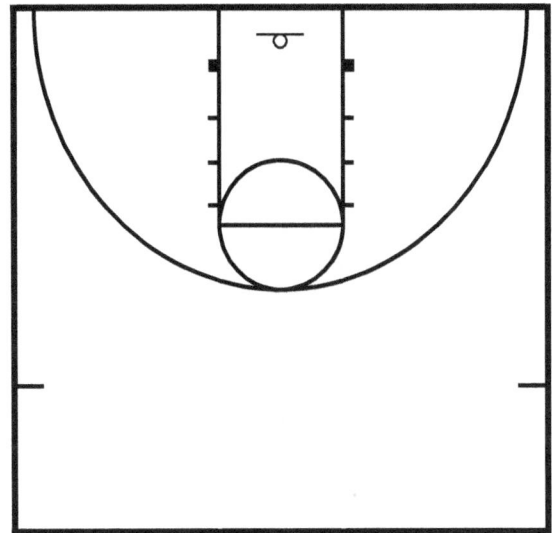

WHEN SHOULD THIS PLAY BE USED?

WHY IS THIS PLAY EFFECTIVE?

WHAT IS MY ROLE IN THIS PLAY?

WHAT KIND OF TEAM DO WE USE THIS PLAY AGAINST?

NAME OF PLAY:

TYPE:

OFFENSIVE   DEFENSIVE

IN WORDS, DESCRIBE THIS PLAY:

WHEN SHOULD THIS PLAY BE USED?

WHY IS THIS PLAY EFFECTIVE?

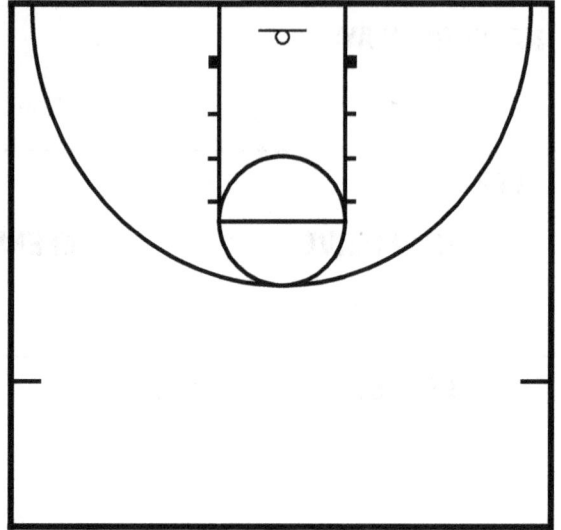

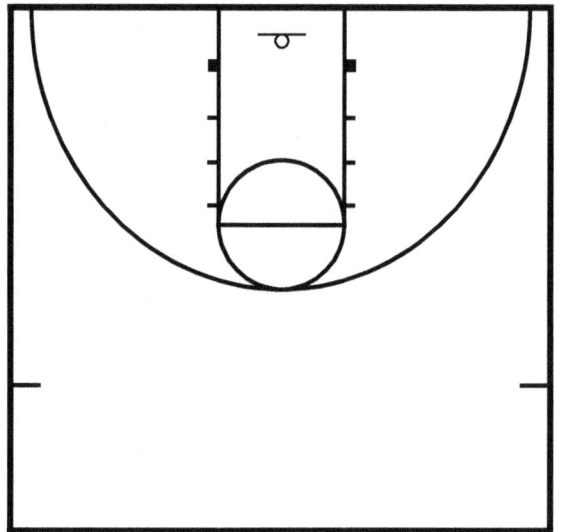

WHAT IS MY ROLE IN THIS PLAY?

WHAT KIND OF TEAM DO WE USE THIS PLAY AGAINST?

NAME OF PLAY:

TYPE:

      OFFENSIVE   **DEFENSIVE**

IN WORDS, DESCRIBE THIS PLAY:

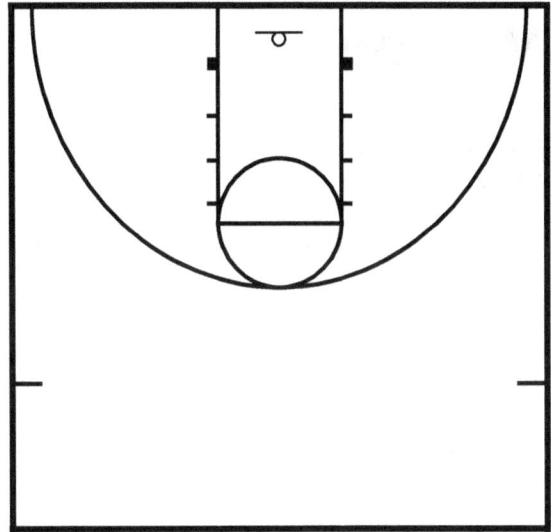

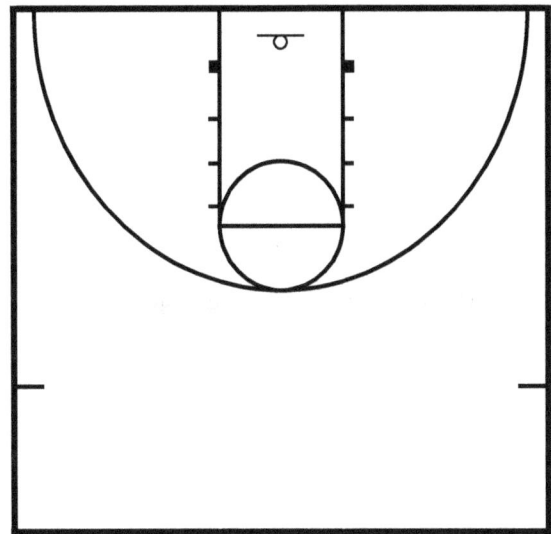

WHEN SHOULD THIS PLAY BE USED?

WHY IS THIS PLAY EFFECTIVE?

WHAT IS MY ROLE IN THIS PLAY?

WHAT KIND OF TEAM DO WE USE THIS PLAY AGAINST?

NAME OF PLAY:

- -

TYPE:

      OFFENSIVE   **DEFENSIVE**

IN WORDS, DESCRIBE THIS PLAY:

- -

WHEN SHOULD THIS PLAY BE USED?

WHAT IS MY ROLE IN THIS PLAY?

- -

WHY IS THIS PLAY EFFECTIVE?

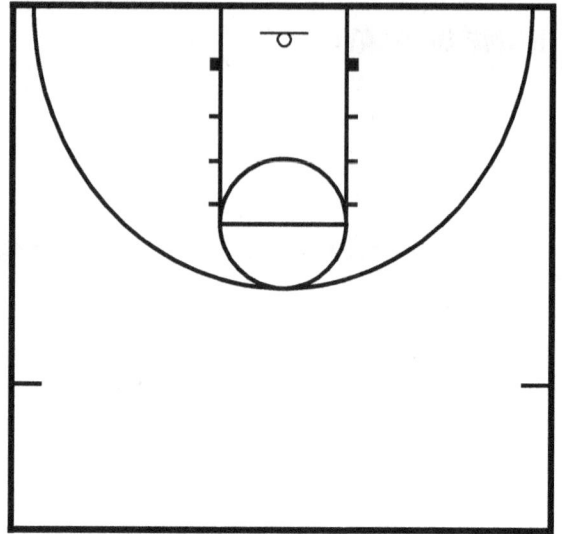

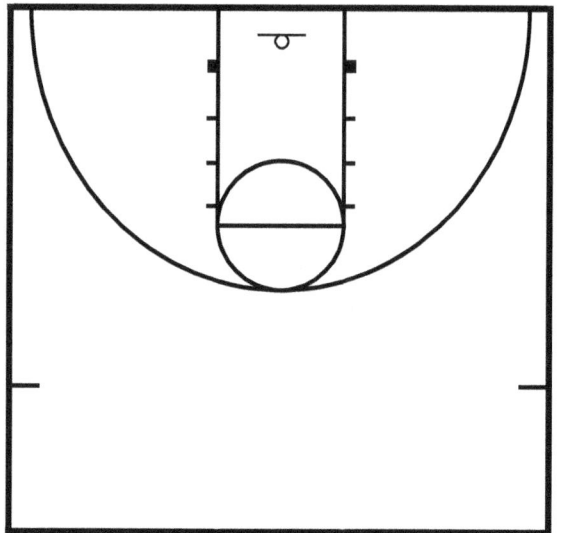

- -

**WHAT KIND OF TEAM DO WE USE
THIS PLAY AGAINST?**

NAME OF PLAY:

TYPE:

      OFFENSIVE   **DEFENSIVE**

IN WORDS, DESCRIBE THIS PLAY:

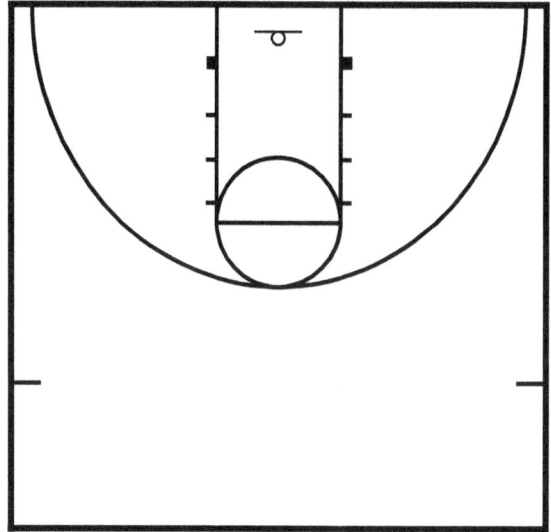

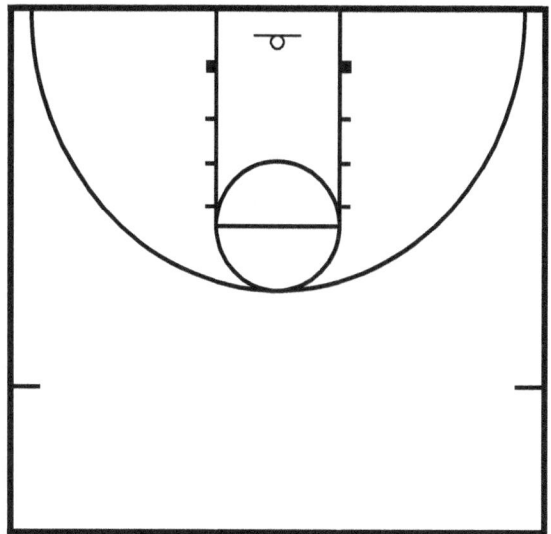

WHEN SHOULD THIS PLAY BE USED?

WHY IS THIS PLAY EFFECTIVE?

WHAT IS MY ROLE IN THIS PLAY?

WHAT KIND OF TEAM DO WE USE THIS PLAY AGAINST?

NAME OF PLAY:

TYPE:

OFFENSIVE   DEFENSIVE

IN WORDS, DESCRIBE THIS PLAY:

WHEN SHOULD THIS PLAY BE USED?

WHY IS THIS PLAY EFFECTIVE?

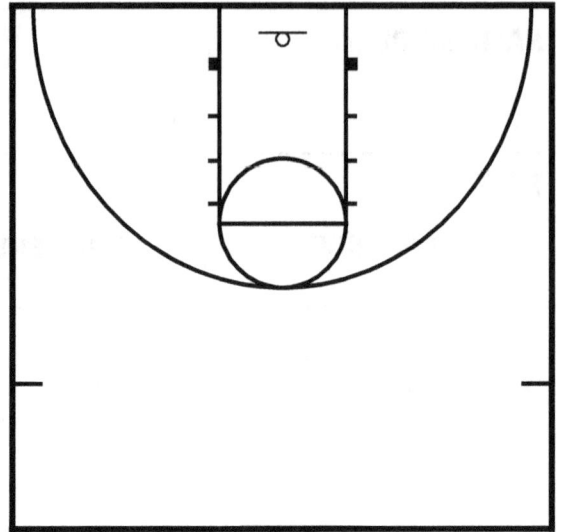

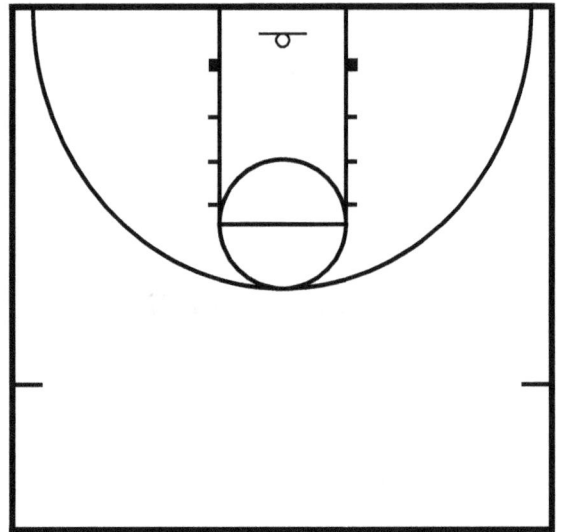

WHAT IS MY ROLE IN THIS PLAY?

WHAT KIND OF TEAM DO WE USE
THIS PLAY AGAINST?

NAME OF PLAY:

TYPE:

OFFENSIVE   **DEFENSIVE**

IN WORDS, DESCRIBE THIS PLAY:

WHEN SHOULD THIS PLAY BE USED?

WHY IS THIS PLAY EFFECTIVE?

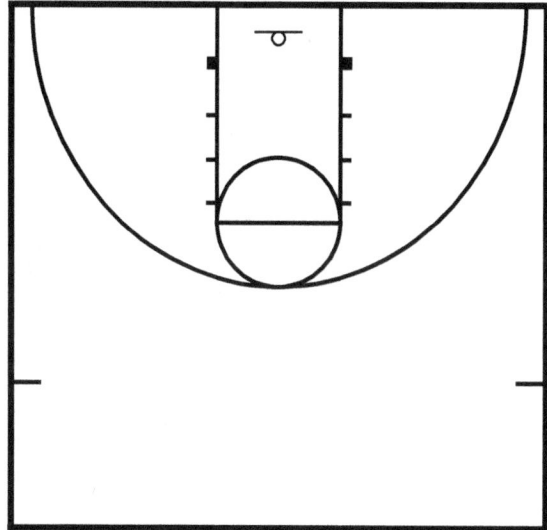

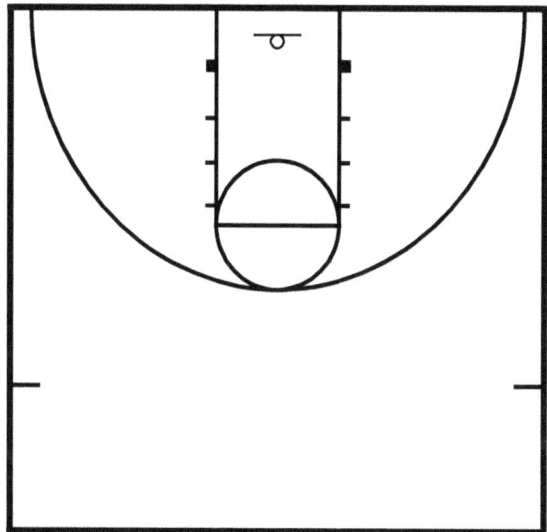

WHAT IS MY ROLE IN THIS PLAY?

WHAT KIND OF TEAM DO WE USE THIS PLAY AGAINST?

Weekly Planning

WEEK #1: _____

WEEKLY SCHEDULE	MY 1% TO DO LIST	MY CHECKLISTS
MONDAY	**GOAL #1**	**PRACTICE-PREP**
		GEAR/SHOES:
		NUTRITION:
TUESDAY		RIDES:
		TREATMENT:
		ASSIGNMENTS:
WEDNESDAY	**GOAL #2**	**GAME-PREP**
		GEAR/SHOES:
THURSDAY		NUTRITION:
		RIDES:
		TREATMENT:
FRIDAY		MENTAL:
	GOAL #3	**SCHOOL**
SATURDAY		HOMEWORK:
		TESTS/QUIZZES:
		ATTENDANCE:
SUNDAY		OTHER:

Weekly Planning

_____ _____ _____

42

WEEK #2: _____

WEEKLY SCHEDULE	MY 1% TO DO LIST	MY CHECKLISTS

WEEKLY SCHEDULE

MONDAY

- - - - - - - - - - - - - - -

TUESDAY

- - - - - - - - - - - - - - -

WEDNESDAY

- - - - - - - - - - - - - - -

THURSDAY

- - - - - - - - - - - - - - -

FRIDAY

- - - - - - - - - - - - - - -

SATURDAY

- - - - - - - - - - - - - - -

SUNDAY

MY 1% TO DO LIST

GOAL #1

- - - - - - - - - - - - - - -

GOAL #2

- - - - - - - - - - - - - - -

GOAL #3

MY CHECKLISTS

PRACTICE-PREP
GEAR/SHOES:

NUTRITION:

RIDES:

TREATMENT:

ASSIGNMENTS:

- - - - - - - - - - - - - - -

GAME-PREP
GEAR/SHOES:

NUTRITION:

RIDES:

TREATMENT:

MENTAL:

- - - - - - - - - - - - - - -

SCHOOL
HOMEWORK:

TESTS/QUIZZES:

ATTENDANCE:

OTHER:

WEEK #3: _____

DATES

WEEKLY SCHEDULE	MY 1% TO DO LIST	MY CHECKLISTS

Weekly Planning

WEEKLY SCHEDULE

MONDAY

TUESDAY

WEDNESDAY

THURSDAY

FRIDAY

SATURDAY

SUNDAY

MY 1% TO DO LIST

GOAL #1

GOAL #2

GOAL #3

MY CHECKLISTS

PRACTICE-PREP
GEAR/SHOES:

NUTRITION:

RIDES:

TREATMENT:

ASSIGNMENTS:

GAME-PREP
GEAR/SHOES:

NUTRITION:

RIDES:

TREATMENT:

MENTAL:

SCHOOL
HOMEWORK:

TESTS/QUIZZES:

ATTENDANCE:

OTHER:

WEEK #4: _____

WEEKLY SCHEDULE	MY 1% TO DO LIST	MY CHECKLISTS

MONDAY

GOAL #1

PRACTICE-PREP
GEAR/SHOES:

NUTRITION:

TUESDAY

RIDES:

TREATMENT:

ASSIGNMENTS:

WEDNESDAY

GOAL #2

GAME-PREP
GEAR/SHOES:

NUTRITION:

THURSDAY

RIDES:

TREATMENT:

FRIDAY

MENTAL:

GOAL #3

SCHOOL
HOMEWORK:

SATURDAY

TESTS/QUIZZES:

ATTENDANCE:

SUNDAY

OTHER:

Weekly Planning

WEEK #5:

WEEKLY SCHEDULE	MY 1% TO DO LIST	MY CHECKLISTS

MONDAY

GOAL #1

PRACTICE-PREP
GEAR/SHOES:

NUTRITION:

TUESDAY

RIDES:

TREATMENT:

ASSIGNMENTS:

WEDNESDAY

GOAL #2

GAME-PREP
GEAR/SHOES:

NUTRITION:

THURSDAY

RIDES:

TREATMENT:

FRIDAY

MENTAL:

GOAL #3

SCHOOL
HOMEWORK:

SATURDAY

TESTS/QUIZZES:

ATTENDANCE:

SUNDAY

OTHER:

Weekly Planning

WEEK #6: _____

WEEKLY SCHEDULE	MY 1% TO DO LIST	MY CHECKLISTS
MONDAY	**GOAL #1**	**PRACTICE-PREP**
		GEAR/SHOES:
		NUTRITION:
TUESDAY		RIDES:
		TREATMENT:
		ASSIGNMENTS:
WEDNESDAY		
	GOAL #2	**GAME-PREP**
		GEAR/SHOES:
THURSDAY		NUTRITION:
		RIDES:
		TREATMENT:
FRIDAY		MENTAL:
	GOAL #3	**SCHOOL**
SATURDAY		HOMEWORK:
		TESTS/QUIZZES:
		ATTENDANCE:
SUNDAY		OTHER:

WEEK #7:

Weekly Planning

WEEKLY SCHEDULE	MY 1% TO DO LIST	MY CHECKLISTS
MONDAY	GOAL #1	PRACTICE-PREP GEAR/SHOES:
		NUTRITION:
TUESDAY		RIDES:
		TREATMENT:
		ASSIGNMENTS:
WEDNESDAY	GOAL #2	GAME-PREP GEAR/SHOES:
THURSDAY		NUTRITION:
		RIDES:
		TREATMENT:
FRIDAY		MENTAL:
	GOAL #3	SCHOOL HOMEWORK:
SATURDAY		TESTS/QUIZZES:
		ATTENDANCE:
SUNDAY		OTHER:

WEEK #8: _____

WEEKLY SCHEDULE	MY 1% TO DO LIST	MY CHECKLISTS

MONDAY

GOAL #1

PRACTICE-PREP
GEAR/SHOES:

NUTRITION:

- - - - - - - - - - - - - - -

TUESDAY

RIDES:

TREATMENT:

ASSIGNMENTS:

- - - - - - - - - - - - - - -

WEDNESDAY

- - - - - - - - - - - - - - -

GOAL #2

GAME-PREP
GEAR/SHOES:

NUTRITION:

- - - - - - - - - - - - - - -

THURSDAY

RIDES:

TREATMENT:

- - - - - - - - - - - - - - -

FRIDAY

MENTAL:

- - - - - - - - - - - - - - -

GOAL #3

SCHOOL
HOMEWORK:

- - - - - - - - - - - - - - -

SATURDAY

TESTS/QUIZZES:

ATTENDANCE:

- - - - - - - - - - - - - - -

SUNDAY

OTHER:

Weekly Planning

WEEK #9: _____

WEEKLY SCHEDULE	MY 1% TO DO LIST	MY CHECKLISTS
MONDAY	GOAL #1	PRACTICE-PREP GEAR/SHOES:
		NUTRITION:
TUESDAY		RIDES:
		TREATMENT:
		ASSIGNMENTS:
WEDNESDAY	GOAL #2	GAME-PREP GEAR/SHOES:
		NUTRITION:
THURSDAY		RIDES:
		TREATMENT:
FRIDAY		MENTAL:
	GOAL #3	SCHOOL HOMEWORK:
SATURDAY		TESTS/QUIZZES:
		ATTENDANCE:
SUNDAY		OTHER:

Weekly Planning

WEEK #10: _____

WEEKLY SCHEDULE	MY 1% TO DO LIST	MY CHECKLISTS
MONDAY	**GOAL #1**	**PRACTICE-PREP**
		GEAR/SHOES:
		NUTRITION:
TUESDAY		**RIDES:**
		TREATMENT:
		ASSIGNMENTS:
WEDNESDAY		
	GOAL #2	**GAME-PREP**
		GEAR/SHOES:
		NUTRITION:
THURSDAY		**RIDES:**
		TREATMENT:
FRIDAY		**MENTAL:**
	GOAL #3	**SCHOOL**
		HOMEWORK:
SATURDAY		**TESTS/QUIZZES:**
		ATTENDANCE:
SUNDAY		**OTHER:**

Weekly Planning

WEEK #11: _____

WEEKLY SCHEDULE	MY 1% TO DO LIST	MY CHECKLISTS

MONDAY

GOAL #1

PRACTICE-PREP
GEAR/SHOES:

NUTRITION:

TUESDAY

RIDES:

TREATMENT:

ASSIGNMENTS:

WEDNESDAY

GOAL #2

GAME-PREP
GEAR/SHOES:

NUTRITION:

THURSDAY

RIDES:

TREATMENT:

FRIDAY

MENTAL:

GOAL #3

SCHOOL
HOMEWORK:

SATURDAY

TESTS/QUIZZES:

ATTENDANCE:

SUNDAY

OTHER:

WEEK #12: _____

WEEKLY SCHEDULE	MY 1% TO DO LIST	MY CHECKLISTS

MONDAY

TUESDAY

WEDNESDAY

THURSDAY

FRIDAY

SATURDAY

SUNDAY

GOAL #1

GOAL #2

GOAL #3

PRACTICE-PREP
GEAR/SHOES:

NUTRITION:

RIDES:

TREATMENT:

ASSIGNMENTS:

GAME-PREP
GEAR/SHOES:

NUTRITION:

RIDES:

TREATMENT:

MENTAL:

SCHOOL
HOMEWORK:

TESTS/QUIZZES:

ATTENDANCE:

OTHER:

Weekly Planning

WEEK #13: _____

DATES

WEEKLY SCHEDULE	MY 1% TO DO LIST	MY CHECKLISTS

WEEKLY SCHEDULE

MONDAY

- - - - - - - - - - - - - - - - - -

TUESDAY

- - - - - - - - - - - - - - - - - -

WEDNESDAY

THURSDAY

- - - - - - - - - - - - - - - - - -

FRIDAY

SATURDAY

- - - - - - - - - - - - - - - - - -

SUNDAY

_____

MY 1% TO DO LIST

GOAL #1

- - - - - - - - - - - - - - - - - -

GOAL #2

- - - - - - - - - - - - - - - - - -

GOAL #3

_____

MY CHECKLISTS

PRACTICE-PREP
GEAR/SHOES:

NUTRITION:

RIDES:

TREATMENT:

ASSIGNMENTS:

- - - - - - - - - - - - - - - - - -

GAME-PREP
GEAR/SHOES:

NUTRITION:

RIDES:

TREATMENT:

MENTAL:

- - - - - - - - - - - - - - - - - -

SCHOOL
HOMEWORK:

TESTS/QUIZZES:

ATTENDANCE:

OTHER:

_____

Weekly Planning

WEEK #14: _____

WEEKLY SCHEDULE

MONDAY

- - - - - - - - - - - - - - - - -

TUESDAY

- - - - - - - - - - - - - - - - -

WEDNESDAY

- - - - - - - - - - - - - - - - -

THURSDAY

- - - - - - - - - - - - - - - - -

FRIDAY

- - - - - - - - - - - - - - - - -

SATURDAY

- - - - - - - - - - - - - - - - -

SUNDAY

MY 1% TO DO LIST

GOAL #1

- -

GOAL #2

- -

GOAL #3

MY CHECKLISTS

PRACTICE-PREP
GEAR/SHOES:

NUTRITION:

RIDES:

TREATMENT:

ASSIGNMENTS:

- - - - - - - - - - - - - - - - -

GAME-PREP
GEAR/SHOES:

NUTRITION:

RIDES:

TREATMENT:

MENTAL:

- - - - - - - - - - - - - - - - -

SCHOOL
HOMEWORK:

TESTS/QUIZZES:

ATTENDANCE:

OTHER:

Weekly Planning

WEEK #15:

WEEKLY SCHEDULE	MY 1% TO DO LIST	MY CHECKLISTS
MONDAY	**GOAL #1**	**PRACTICE-PREP** GEAR/SHOES:
		NUTRITION:
TUESDAY		RIDES:
		TREATMENT:
		ASSIGNMENTS:
WEDNESDAY	**GOAL #2**	**GAME-PREP** GEAR/SHOES:
		NUTRITION:
THURSDAY		RIDES:
		TREATMENT:
FRIDAY		MENTAL:
	GOAL #3	**SCHOOL** HOMEWORK:
SATURDAY		TESTS/QUIZZES:
		ATTENDANCE:
SUNDAY		OTHER:

Weekly Planning

WEEK #16: _____

WEEKLY SCHEDULE	MY 1% TO DO LIST	MY CHECKLISTS

MONDAY

GOAL #1

PRACTICE-PREP
GEAR/SHOES:

NUTRITION:

TUESDAY

RIDES:

TREATMENT:

ASSIGNMENTS:

WEDNESDAY

GOAL #2

GAME-PREP
GEAR/SHOES:

NUTRITION:

THURSDAY

RIDES:

TREATMENT:

FRIDAY

MENTAL:

GOAL #3

SCHOOL
HOMEWORK:

SATURDAY

TESTS/QUIZZES:

ATTENDANCE:

SUNDAY

OTHER:

Film & Scouting Reports

FILM & SCOUTING REPORT

HOME:
GUEST:

DATE:
ASSIGNED COACH:
ASSIGNED PLAYER:

HOME

SCORE: 1ST____ 2ND____ 3RD____ 4TH____

MAN: Y OR N
ZONE SETS:

PRESS: Y OR N
DETAILS:

OFFENSE SETS:

SHOT CHART:

Q1   Q2

Q3   Q4

#	REBs	FLs	STs	TOs	#	REBs	FLs	STs	TOs

GUEST

SCORE: 1ST____ 2ND____ 3RD____ 4TH____

MAN: Y OR N
ZONE SETS:

PRESS: Y OR N
DETAILS:

OFFENSE SETS:

SHOT CHART:

Q1   Q2

Q3   Q4

#	REBs	FLs	STs	TOs	#	REBs	FLs	STs	TOs

Film & Scouting

FOR SCOUTING REPORTS:
WHO ARE THE KEY PERSONNEL TO KNOW OF? WHY?

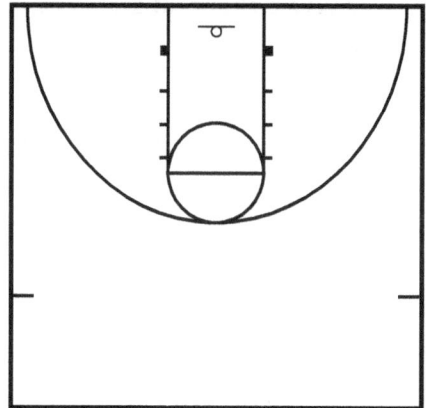

WHAT ARE OUR LIKELY MATCHUPS?

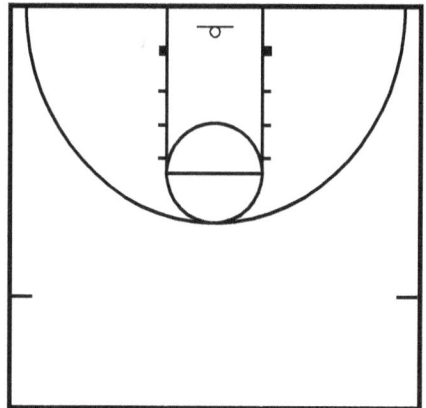

DO THEY LIKE TO RUN?	YES OR **NO**
WHERE DO THEY SHOOT FROM?	LEFT, RIGHT, OR **BOTH**
DO THEY ATTACK THE BASKET?	YES OR **NO**
DO THEY PRESS?	YES OR **NO**
IS MAN DEFENSE:	TIGHT OR **SAGGING**

HOW DO THEY DEFEND THE POST? FORWARDS?

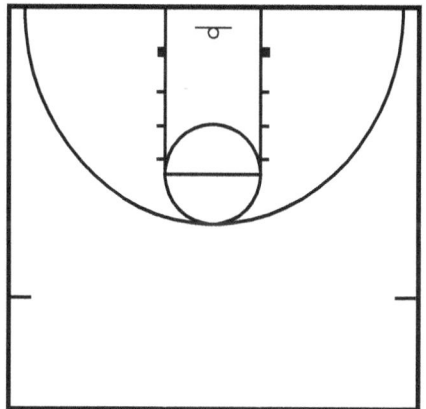

DEFENSIVE WEAK POINTS? PRESS WEAK POINTS?

HOW DO WE COMBAT THEIR OFFENSIVE APPROACH?

HOW DO WE COMBAT THEIR DEFENSIVE APPROACH?

HOW WILL I DARE GREATLY? HOW WILL I IMPROVE ON MY 1% GOALS?

Film & Scouting

FILM &
SCOUTING REPORT

HOME:

GUEST:

DATE:

ASSIGNED COACH:

ASSIGNED PLAYER:

HOME

GUEST

SCORE:	1ST____	2ND____	3RD____	4TH____	

MAN: Y or N
ZONE SETS:

PRESS: Y or N
DETAILS:

SCORE:	1ST____	2ND____	3RD____	4TH____	

MAN: Y or N
ZONE SETS:

PRESS: Y or N
DETAILS:

OFFENSE SETS:

OFFENSE SETS:

SHOT CHART:

Q1   Q2

Q3   Q4

SHOT CHART:

Q1   Q2

Q3   Q4

#	REBs	FLs	STs	TOs	#	REBs	FLs	STs	TOs

#	REBs	FLs	STs	TOs	#	REBs	FLs	STs	TOs

FOR SCOUTING REPORTS:
   WHO ARE THE KEY PERSONNEL TO KNOW OF? WHY?

WHAT ARE OUR LIKELY MATCHUPS?

DO THEY LIKE TO RUN?	YES OR NO
WHERE DO THEY SHOOT FROM?	LEFT, RIGHT, OR BOTH
DO THEY ATTACK THE BASKET?	YES OR NO
DO THEY PRESS?	YES OR NO
IS MAN DEFENSE:	TIGHT OR SAGGING

HOW DO THEY DEFEND THE POST? FORWARDS?

DEFENSIVE WEAK POINTS? PRESS WEAK POINTS?

WHICH PLAYS SHOULD WE USE AGAINST THIS TEAM?

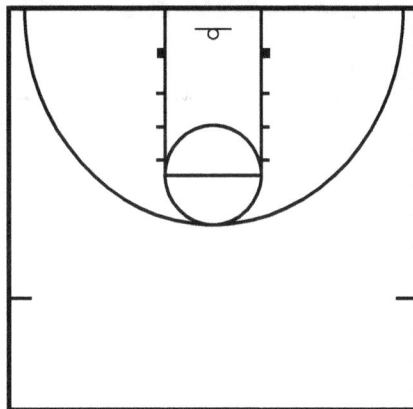

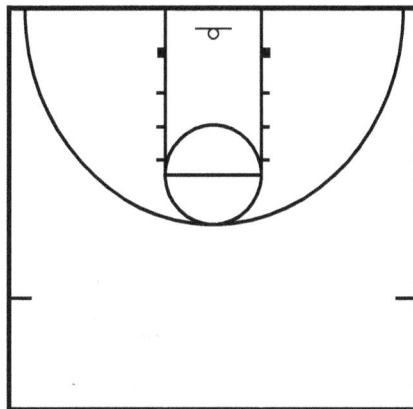

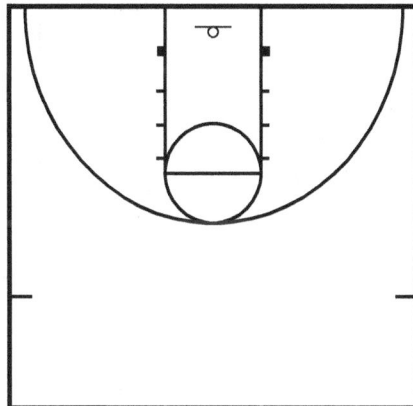

HOW DO WE COMBAT THEIR OFFENSIVE APPROACH?

HOW DO WE COMBAT THEIR DEFENSIVE APPROACH?

HOW WILL I DARE GREATLY? HOW WILL I IMPROVE ON MY 1% GOALS?

FILM & SCOUTING REPORT

HOME:

GUEST:

DATE:

ASSIGNED COACH:

ASSIGNED PLAYER:

HOME

| SCORE: | 1ST____ | 2ND____ | 3RD____ | 4TH____ |

MAN: Y OR N

ZONE SETS:

PRESS: Y OR N

DETAILS:

OFFENSE SETS:

SHOT CHART:

Q1   Q2

Q3   Q4

GUEST

| SCORE: | 1ST____ | 2ND____ | 3RD____ | 4TH____ |

MAN: Y OR N

ZONE SETS:

PRESS: Y OR N

DETAILS:

OFFENSE SETS:

SHOT CHART:

Q1   Q2

Q3   Q4

#	REBs	FLs	STs	TOs	#	REBs	FLs	STs	TOs	#	REBs	FLs	STs	TOs	#	REBs	FLs	STs	TOs

Film & Scouting

64

FOR SCOUTING REPORTS:
WHO ARE THE KEY PERSONNEL TO KNOW OF? WHY?

WHAT ARE OUR LIKELY MATCHUPS?

WHICH PLAYS SHOULD WE USE AGAINST THIS TEAM?

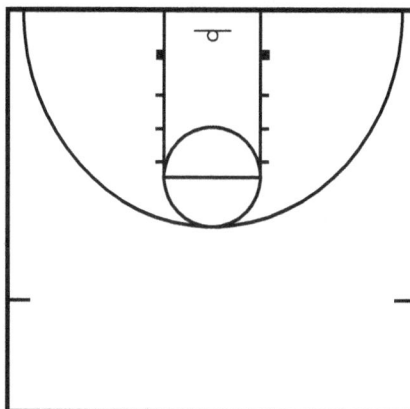

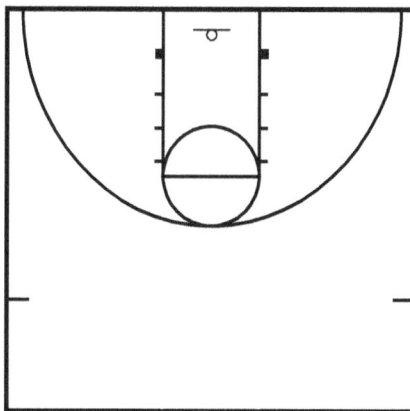

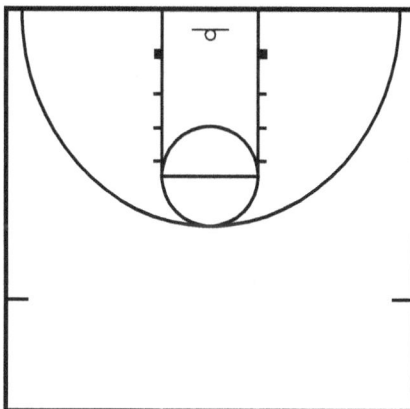

DO THEY LIKE TO RUN?   YES OR **NO**
WHERE DO THEY SHOOT FROM?   LEFT, RIGHT, OR **BOTH**
DO THEY ATTACK THE BASKET?   YES OR **NO**
DO THEY PRESS?   YES OR **NO**
IS MAN DEFENSE: TIGHT OR **SAGGING**

HOW DO THEY DEFEND THE POST? FORWARDS?

DEFENSIVE WEAK POINTS? PRESS WEAK POINTS?

HOW DO WE COMBAT THEIR OFFENSIVE APPROACH?

HOW DO WE COMBAT THEIR DEFENSIVE APPROACH?

HOW WILL I DARE GREATLY? HOW WILL I IMPROVE ON MY 1% GOALS?

Film & Scouting

FILM & SCOUTING REPORT

HOME: _____ DATE: ___ ASSIGNED COACH: _____

GUEST: _____ ___ ASSIGNED PLAYER: _____

HOME

| SCORE: | 1ST____ | 2ND____ | 3RD____ | 4TH____ |

MAN: Y OR N
ZONE SETS:

PRESS: Y OR N
DETAILS:

OFFENSE SETS:

SHOT CHART:

Q1   Q2

Q3   Q4

#	REBs	FLs	STs	TOs	#	REBs	FLs	STs	TOs

GUEST

| SCORE: | 1ST____ | 2ND____ | 3RD____ | 4TH____ |

MAN: Y OR N
ZONE SETS:

PRESS: Y OR N
DETAILS:

OFFENSE SETS:

SHOT CHART:

Q1   Q2

Q3   Q4

#	REBs	FLs	STs	TOs	#	REBs	FLs	STs	TOs

FOR SCOUTING REPORTS:
WHO ARE THE KEY PERSONNEL TO KNOW OF? WHY?

WHICH PLAYS SHOULD WE USE AGAINST THIS TEAM?

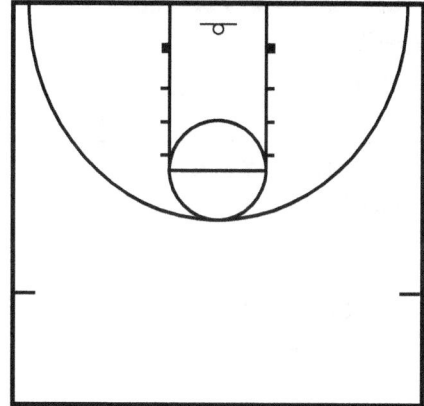

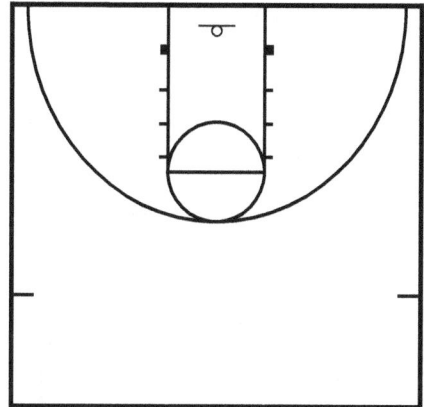

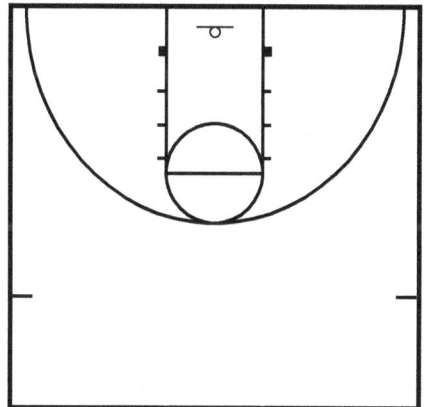

WHAT ARE OUR LIKELY MATCHUPS?

DO THEY LIKE TO RUN?	YES or NO
WHERE DO THEY SHOOT FROM?	LEFT, RIGHT, or BOTH
DO THEY ATTACK THE BASKET?	YES or NO
DO THEY PRESS?	YES or NO
IS MAN DEFENSE:	TIGHT or SAGGING

HOW DO THEY DEFEND THE POST? FORWARDS?

DEFENSIVE WEAK POINTS? PRESS WEAK POINTS?

HOW DO WE COMBAT THEIR OFFENSIVE APPROACH?

HOW DO WE COMBAT THEIR DEFENSIVE APPROACH?

HOW WILL I DARE GREATLY? HOW WILL I IMPROVE ON MY 1% GOALS?

FILM &
SCOUTING REPORT

HOME:

GUEST:

DATE:

ASSIGNED COACH:

ASSIGNED PLAYER:

HOME

GUEST

SCORE: | 1ST_____ 2ND_____ 3RD_____ 4TH_____

MAN: | Y OR N
ZONE SETS: |

PRESS: | Y OR N
DETAILS: |

OFFENSE
SETS: |

SHOT
CHART: |

Q1   Q2

Q3   Q4

SCORE: | 1ST_____ 2ND_____ 3RD_____ 4TH_____

MAN: | Y OR N
ZONE SETS: |

PRESS: | Y OR N
DETAILS: |

OFFENSE
SETS: |

SHOT
CHART: |

Q1   Q2

Q3   Q4

#	REBs	FLs	STs	TOs	#	REBs	FLs	STs	TOs	#	REBs	FLs	STs	TOs	#	REBs	FLs	STs	TOs

Film & Scouting

68

FOR SCOUTING REPORTS:
WHO ARE THE KEY PERSONNEL TO KNOW OF? WHY?

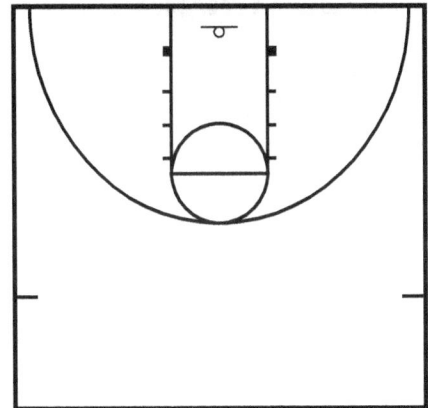

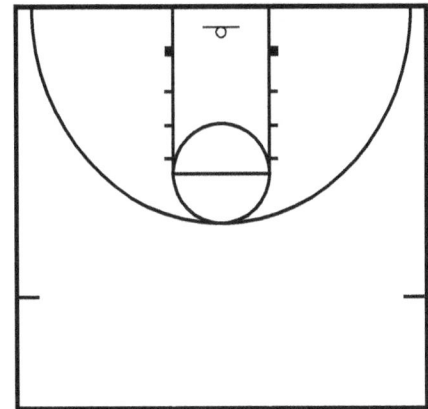

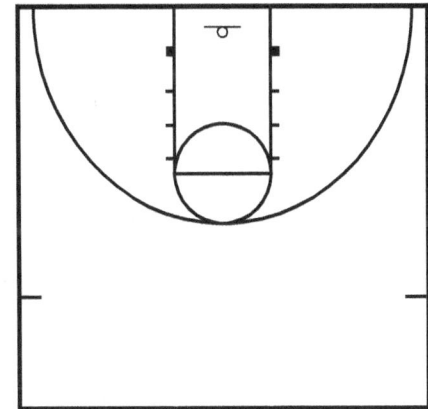

WHAT ARE OUR LIKELY MATCHUPS?

DO THEY LIKE TO RUN?	YES or NO
WHERE DO THEY SHOOT FROM?	LEFT, RIGHT, or BOTH
DO THEY ATTACK THE BASKET?	YES or NO
DO THEY PRESS?	YES or NO
IS MAN DEFENSE:	TIGHT or SAGGING

HOW DO THEY DEFEND THE POST? FORWARDS?

DEFENSIVE WEAK POINTS? PRESS WEAK POINTS?

HOW DO WE COMBAT THEIR OFFENSIVE APPROACH?

HOW DO WE COMBAT THEIR DEFENSIVE APPROACH?

HOW WILL I DARE GREATLY? HOW WILL I IMPROVE ON MY 1% GOALS?

Film & Scouting

FILM & SCOUTING REPORT

HOME:

GUEST:

DATE:

ASSIGNED COACH:

ASSIGNED PLAYER:

HOME

SCORE: 1ST____ 2ND____ 3RD____ 4TH____

MAN: Y or N
ZONE SETS:

PRESS: Y or N
DETAILS:

OFFENSE SETS:

SHOT CHART:

Q1 Q2 Q3 Q4

#	REBs	FLs	STs	TOs	#	REBs	FLs	STs	TOs

GUEST

SCORE: 1ST____ 2ND____ 3RD____ 4TH____

MAN: Y or N
ZONE SETS:

PRESS: Y or N
DETAILS:

OFFENSE SETS:

SHOT CHART:

Q1 Q2 Q3 Q4

#	REBs	FLs	STs	TOs	#	REBs	FLs	STs	TOs

Film & Scouting

FOR SCOUTING REPORTS:
WHO ARE THE KEY PERSONNEL TO KNOW OF? WHY?

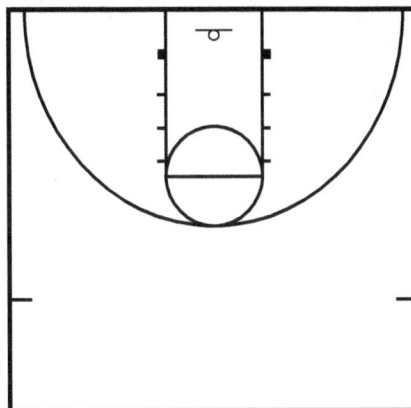

WHAT ARE OUR LIKELY MATCHUPS?

DO THEY LIKE TO RUN?	**YES** OR **NO**
WHERE DO THEY SHOOT FROM?	**LEFT, RIGHT,** OR **BOTH**
DO THEY ATTACK THE BASKET?	**YES** OR **NO**
DO THEY PRESS?	**YES** OR **NO**
IS MAN DEFENSE:	**TIGHT** OR **SAGGING**

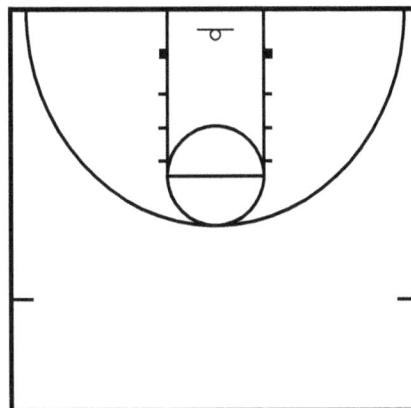

HOW DO THEY DEFEND THE POST? FORWARDS?

DEFENSIVE WEAK POINTS? PRESS WEAK POINTS?

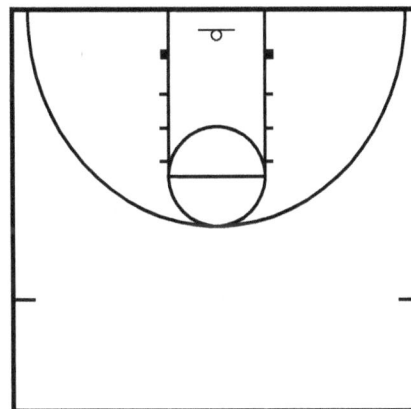

HOW DO WE COMBAT THEIR OFFENSIVE APPROACH?

HOW DO WE COMBAT THEIR DEFENSIVE APPROACH?

HOW WILL I DARE GREATLY? HOW WILL I IMPROVE ON MY 1% GOALS?

Film & Scouting

FILM &
SCOUTING REPORT

HOME:

GUEST:

DATE:

ASSIGNED COACH:

ASSIGNED PLAYER:

SCORE: 1ST____ 2ND____ 3RD____ 4TH____

MAN: Y OR N
ZONE SETS:

PRESS: Y OR N
DETAILS:

OFFENSE
SETS:

SHOT
CHART:

Q1

Q2

Q3

Q4

SCORE: 1ST____ 2ND____ 3RD____ 4TH____

MAN: Y OR N
ZONE SETS:

PRESS: Y OR N
DETAILS:

OFFENSE
SETS:

SHOT
CHART:

Q1

Q2

Q3

Q4

#	REBs	FLs	STs	TOs	#	REBs	FLs	STs	TOs	#	REBs	FLs	STs	TOs	#	REBs	FLs	STs	TOs

Film & Scouting

72

FOR SCOUTING REPORTS:
WHO ARE THE KEY PERSONNEL TO KNOW OF? WHY?

WHAT ARE OUR LIKELY MATCHUPS?

DO THEY LIKE TO RUN?	YES OR **NO**
WHERE DO THEY SHOOT FROM?	LEFT, **RIGHT,** OR BOTH
DO THEY ATTACK THE BASKET?	YES OR **NO**
DO THEY PRESS?	YES OR **NO**
IS MAN DEFENSE:	TIGHT OR **SAGGING**

HOW DO THEY DEFEND THE POST? FORWARDS?

DEFENSIVE WEAK POINTS? PRESS WEAK POINTS?

WHICH PLAYS SHOULD WE USE AGAINST THIS TEAM?

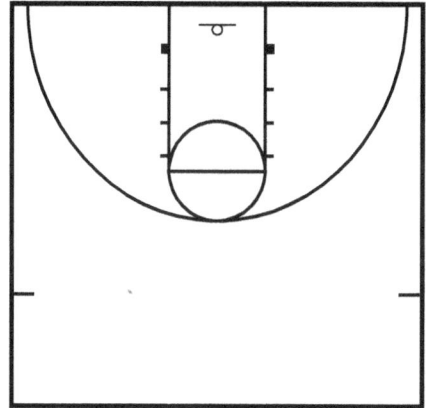

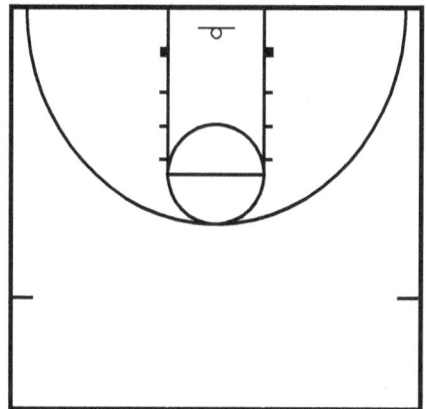

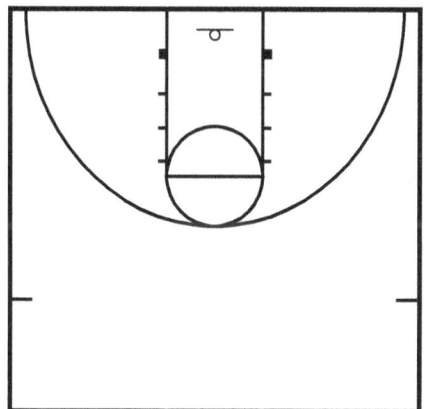

HOW DO WE COMBAT THEIR OFFENSIVE APPROACH?

HOW DO WE COMBAT THEIR DEFENSIVE APPROACH?

HOW WILL I DARE GREATLY? HOW WILL I IMPROVE ON MY 1% GOALS?

Film & Scouting

FILM & SCOUTING REPORT

HOME:

GUEST:

DATE:

ASSIGNED COACH:

ASSIGNED PLAYER:

HOME

GUEST

	HOME		GUEST	
SCORE:	1ST____ 2ND____ 3RD____ 4TH____		SCORE: 1ST____ 2ND____ 3RD____ 4TH____	
MAN: ZONE SETS:	Y or N		MAN: ZONE SETS: Y or N	
PRESS: DETAILS:	Y or N		PRESS: DETAILS: Y or N	

OFFENSE SETS:

OFFENSE SETS:

SHOT CHART:

Q1

Q2

Q3

Q4

SHOT CHART:

Q1

Q2

Q3

Q4

#	REBs	FLs	STs	TOs	#	REBs	FLs	STs	TOs	#	REBs	FLs	STs	TOs	#	REBs	FLs	STs	TOs

FOR SCOUTING REPORTS:
WHO ARE THE KEY PERSONNEL TO KNOW OF? WHY?

WHAT ARE OUR LIKELY MATCHUPS?

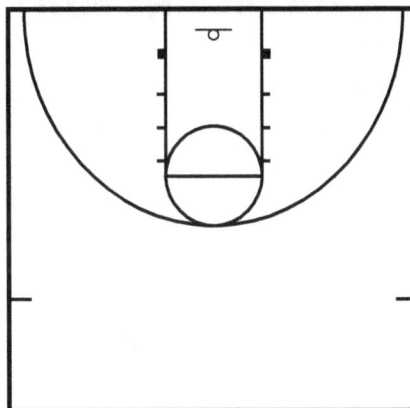

DO THEY LIKE TO RUN?   YES or **NO**
WHERE DO THEY SHOOT FROM?   LEFT, RIGHT, or **BOTH**
DO THEY ATTACK THE BASKET?   YES or **NO**
DO THEY PRESS?   YES or **NO**
IS MAN DEFENSE: TIGHT or **SAGGING**

HOW DO THEY DEFEND THE POST? FORWARDS?

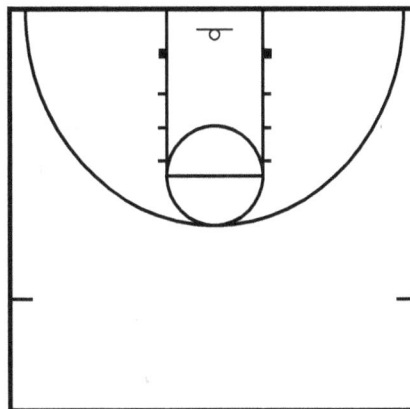

DEFENSIVE WEAK POINTS? PRESS WEAK POINTS?

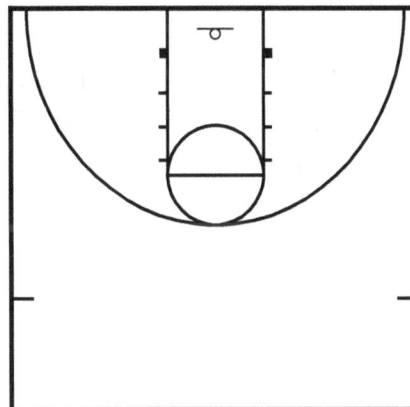

HOW DO WE COMBAT THEIR OFFENSIVE APPROACH?

HOW DO WE COMBAT THEIR DEFENSIVE APPROACH?

HOW WILL I DARE GREATLY? HOW WILL I IMPROVE ON MY 1% GOALS?

Film & Scouting

FILM &
SCOUTING REPORT

HOME:

GUEST:

DATE:

ASSIGNED COACH:

ASSIGNED PLAYER:

HOME

GUEST

SCORE:	1ST____	2ND____	3RD____	4TH____

MAN: Y or N
ZONE SETS:

PRESS: Y or N
DETAILS:

OFFENSE SETS:

SHOT CHART:

Q1   Q2

Q3   Q4

SCORE:	1ST____	2ND____	3RD____	4TH____

MAN: Y or N
ZONE SETS:

PRESS: Y or N
DETAILS:

OFFENSE SETS:

SHOT CHART:

Q1   Q2

Q3   Q4

#	REBs	FLs	STs	TOs	#	REBs	FLs	STs	TOs

#	REBs	FLs	STs	TOs	#	REBs	FLs	STs	TOs

FOR SCOUTING REPORTS:

WHO ARE THE KEY PERSONNEL TO KNOW OF? WHY?

WHAT ARE OUR LIKELY MATCHUPS?

DO THEY LIKE TO RUN?	YES OR NO
WHERE DO THEY SHOOT FROM?	LEFT, RIGHT, OR BOTH
DO THEY ATTACK THE BASKET?	YES OR NO
DO THEY PRESS?	YES OR NO
IS MAN DEFENSE:	TIGHT OR SAGGING

HOW DO THEY DEFEND THE POST? FORWARDS?

DEFENSIVE WEAK POINTS? PRESS WEAK POINTS?

HOW DO WE COMBAT THEIR OFFENSIVE APPROACH?

HOW DO WE COMBAT THEIR DEFENSIVE APPROACH?

HOW WILL I DARE GREATLY? HOW WILL I IMPROVE ON MY 1% GOALS?

WHICH PLAYS SHOULD WE USE AGAINST THIS TEAM?

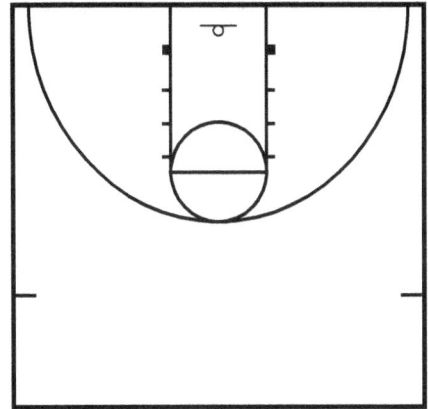

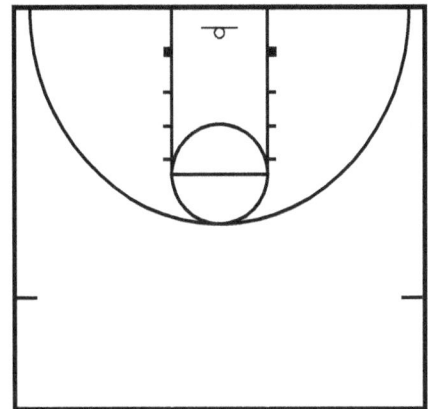

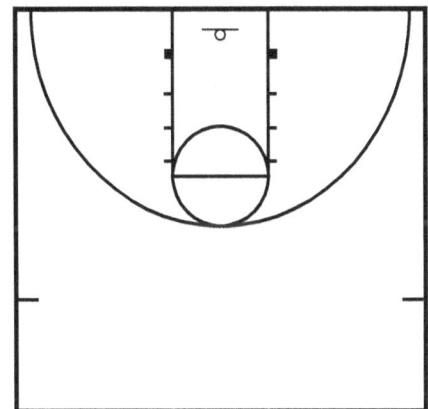

Film & Scouting

FILM & SCOUTING REPORT

HOME:

GUEST:

DATE:

ASSIGNED COACH:

ASSIGNED PLAYER:

HOME

GUEST

	HOME		GUEST	
SCORE:	1ST____ 2ND____ 3RD____ 4TH____		1ST____ 2ND____ 3RD____ 4TH____	

MAN: Y OR N
ZONE SETS:

PRESS: Y OR N
DETAILS:

OFFENSE SETS:

SHOT CHART:

Q1   Q2

Q3   Q4

MAN: Y OR N
ZONE SETS:

PRESS: Y OR N
DETAILS:

OFFENSE SETS:

SHOT CHART:

Q1   Q2

Q3   Q4

#	REBs	FLs	STs	TOs	#	REBs	FLs	STs	TOs	#	REBs	FLs	STs	TOs	#	REBs	FLs	STs	TOs

FOR SCOUTING REPORTS:
WHO ARE THE KEY PERSONNEL TO KNOW OF? WHY?

WHAT ARE OUR LIKELY MATCHUPS?

DO THEY LIKE TO RUN?	YES OR NO
WHERE DO THEY SHOOT FROM?	LEFT, RIGHT, OR BOTH
DO THEY ATTACK THE BASKET?	YES OR NO
DO THEY PRESS?	YES OR NO
IS MAN DEFENSE:	TIGHT OR SAGGING

HOW DO THEY DEFEND THE POST? FORWARDS?

DEFENSIVE WEAK POINTS? PRESS WEAK POINTS?

WHICH PLAYS SHOULD WE USE AGAINST THIS TEAM?

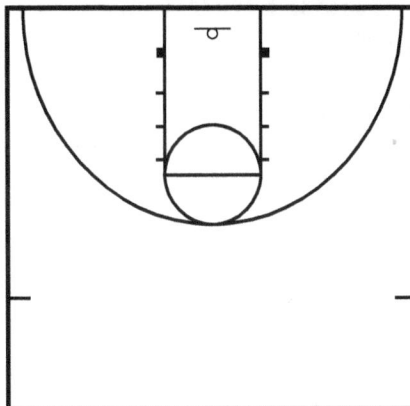

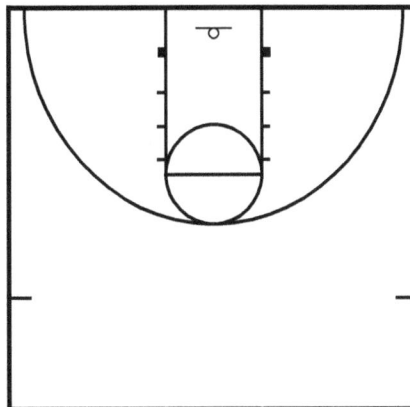

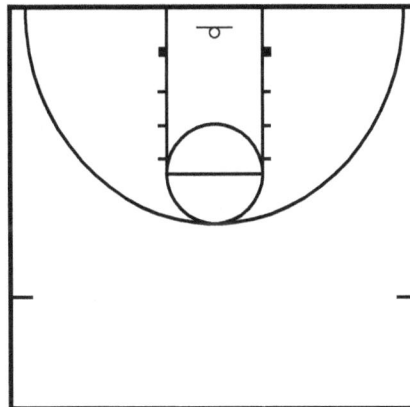

HOW DO WE COMBAT THEIR OFFENSIVE APPROACH?

HOW DO WE COMBAT THEIR DEFENSIVE APPROACH?

HOW WILL I DARE GREATLY? HOW WILL I IMPROVE ON MY 1% GOALS?

FILM & SCOUTING REPORT

HOME:

GUEST:

DATE:

ASSIGNED COACH:

ASSIGNED PLAYER:

HOME

SCORE: 1ST_____ 2ND_____ 3RD_____ 4TH_____

MAN: Y or N

ZONE SETS:

PRESS: Y or N

DETAILS:

OFFENSE SETS:

SHOT CHART:

Q1   Q2

Q3   Q4

#	REBs	FLs	STs	TOs	#	REBs	FLs	STs	TOs

GUEST

SCORE: 1ST_____ 2ND_____ 3RD_____ 4TH_____

MAN: Y or N

ZONE SETS:

PRESS: Y or N

DETAILS:

OFFENSE SETS:

SHOT CHART:

Q1   Q2

Q3   Q4

#	REBs	FLs	STs	TOs	#	REBs	FLs	STs	TOs

Film & Scouting

FOR SCOUTING REPORTS:
WHO ARE THE KEY PERSONNEL TO KNOW OF? WHY?

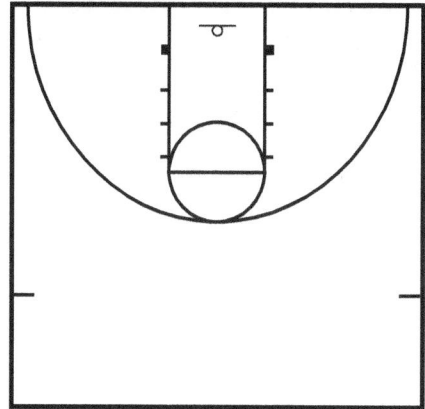

WHAT ARE OUR LIKELY MATCHUPS?

DO THEY LIKE TO RUN?   YES or **NO**

WHERE DO THEY SHOOT FROM?   LEFT, RIGHT, or **BOTH**

DO THEY ATTACK THE BASKET?   YES or **NO**

DO THEY PRESS?   YES or **NO**

IS MAN DEFENSE: TIGHT or **SAGGING**

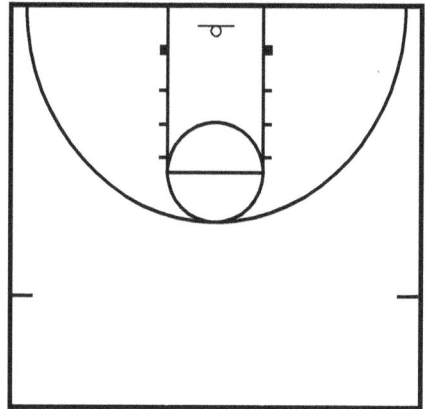

HOW DO THEY DEFEND THE POST? FORWARDS?

DEFENSIVE WEAK POINTS? PRESS WEAK POINTS?

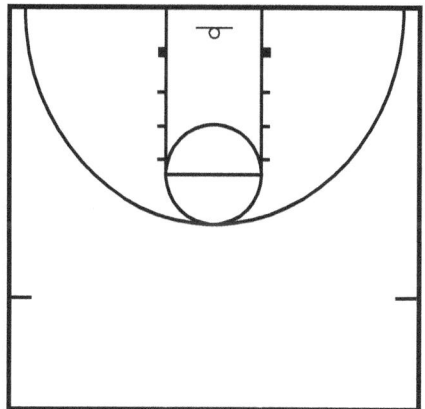

HOW DO WE COMBAT THEIR OFFENSIVE APPROACH?

HOW DO WE COMBAT THEIR DEFENSIVE APPROACH?

HOW WILL I DARE GREATLY? HOW WILL I IMPROVE ON MY 1% GOALS?

FILM & SCOUTING REPORT

HOME: _____ GUEST: _____

DATE: _____

ASSIGNED COACH: _____

ASSIGNED PLAYER: _____

HOME

GUEST

SCORE: 1ST____ 2ND____ 3RD____ 4TH____	**SCORE:** 1ST____ 2ND____ 3RD____ 4TH____
MAN: ZONE SETS: Y or N	**MAN: ZONE SETS:** Y or N
PRESS: DETAILS: Y or N	**PRESS: DETAILS:** Y or N
OFFENSE SETS:	**OFFENSE SETS:**
SHOT CHART: Q1 Q2 Q3 Q4	**SHOT CHART:** Q1 Q2 Q3 Q4

#	REBs	FLs	STs	TOs	#	REBs	FLs	STs	TOs	#	REBs	FLs	STs	TOs	#	REBs	FLs	STs	TOs

FOR SCOUTING REPORTS:
WHO ARE THE KEY PERSONNEL TO KNOW OF? WHY?

WHAT ARE OUR LIKELY MATCHUPS?

DO THEY LIKE TO RUN?	YES OR NO
WHERE DO THEY SHOOT FROM?	LEFT, RIGHT, OR BOTH
DO THEY ATTACK THE BASKET?	YES OR NO
DO THEY PRESS?	YES OR NO
IS MAN DEFENSE:	TIGHT OR SAGGING

HOW DO THEY DEFEND THE POST? FORWARDS?

DEFENSIVE WEAK POINTS? PRESS WEAK POINTS?

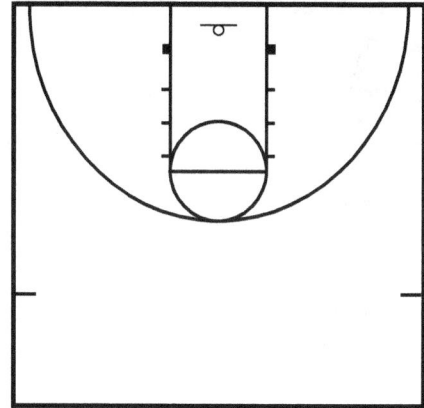

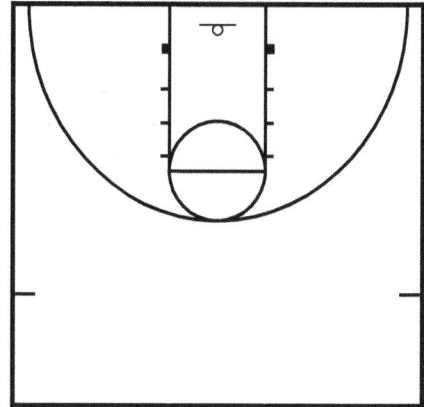

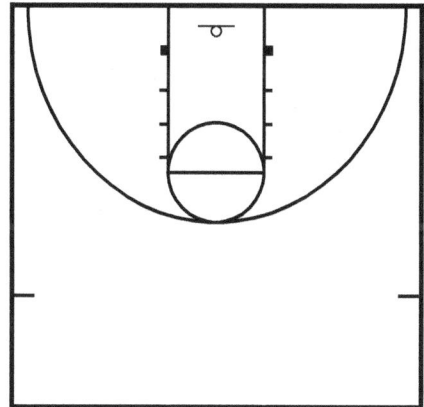

HOW DO WE COMBAT THEIR OFFENSIVE APPROACH?

HOW DO WE COMBAT THEIR DEFENSIVE APPROACH?

HOW WILL I DARE GREATLY? HOW WILL I IMPROVE ON MY 1% GOALS?

FILM & SCOUTING REPORT

HOME: _____ DATE: _____ ASSIGNED COACH: _____

GUEST: _____ ASSIGNED PLAYER: _____

HOME   **GUEST**

HOME		GUEST	

SCORE: 1ST____ 2ND____ 3RD____ 4TH____

MAN: Y OR N
ZONE SETS:

PRESS: Y OR N
DETAILS:

OFFENSE SETS:

SHOT CHART:

Q1   Q2

Q3   Q4

SCORE: 1ST____ 2ND____ 3RD____ 4TH____

MAN: Y OR N
ZONE SETS:

PRESS: Y OR N
DETAILS:

OFFENSE SETS:

SHOT CHART:

Q1   Q2

Q3   Q4

#	REBs	FLs	STs	TOs	#	REBs	FLs	STs	TOs	#	REBs	FLs	STs	TOs	#	REBs	FLs	STs	TOs

FOR SCOUTING REPORTS:
WHO ARE THE KEY PERSONNEL TO KNOW OF? WHY?

WHAT ARE OUR LIKELY MATCHUPS?

WHICH PLAYS SHOULD WE
USE AGAINST THIS TEAM?

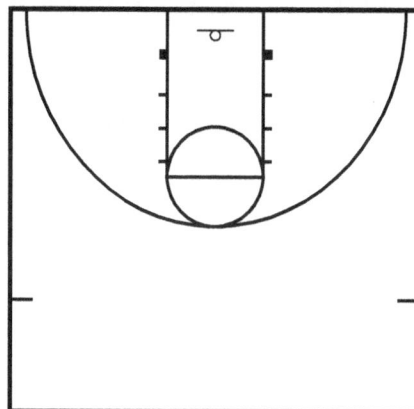

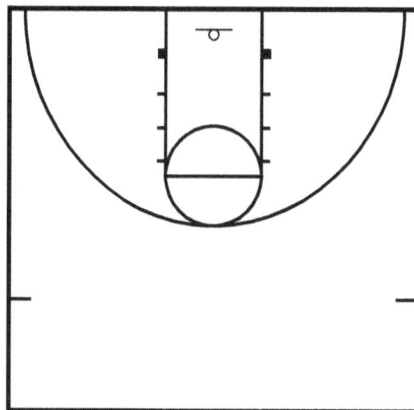

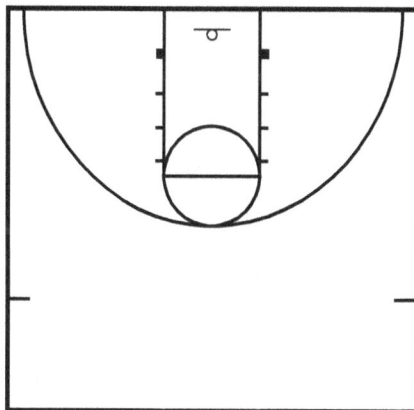

DO THEY LIKE TO RUN?	YES OR NO
WHERE DO THEY SHOOT FROM?	LEFT, RIGHT, OR BOTH
DO THEY ATTACK THE BASKET?	YES OR NO
DO THEY PRESS?	YES OR NO
IS MAN DEFENSE:	TIGHT OR SAGGING

HOW DO THEY DEFEND THE POST? FORWARDS?

DEFENSIVE WEAK POINTS? PRESS WEAK POINTS?

HOW DO WE COMBAT THEIR OFFENSIVE APPROACH?

HOW DO WE COMBAT THEIR DEFENSIVE APPROACH?

HOW WILL I DARE GREATLY? HOW WILL I IMPROVE ON MY 1% GOALS?

Film & Scouting

FILM & SCOUTING REPORT

HOME:
GUEST:

DATE:

ASSIGNED COACH:
ASSIGNED PLAYER:

HOME

GUEST

| SCORE: | 1ST____ | 2ND____ | 3RD____ | 4TH____ |

MAN: Y or N
ZONE SETS:

PRESS: Y or N
DETAILS:

OFFENSE SETS:

SHOT CHART:

Q1   Q2

Q3   Q4

| SCORE: | 1ST____ | 2ND____ | 3RD____ | 4TH____ |

MAN: Y or N
ZONE SETS:

PRESS: Y or N
DETAILS:

OFFENSE SETS:

SHOT CHART:

Q1   Q2

Q3   Q4

#	REBs	FLs	STs	TOs	#	REBs	FLs	STs	TOs	#	REBs	FLs	STs	TOs	#	REBs	FLs	STs	TOs

FOR SCOUTING REPORTS:
WHO ARE THE KEY PERSONNEL TO KNOW OF? WHY?

WHAT ARE OUR LIKELY MATCHUPS?

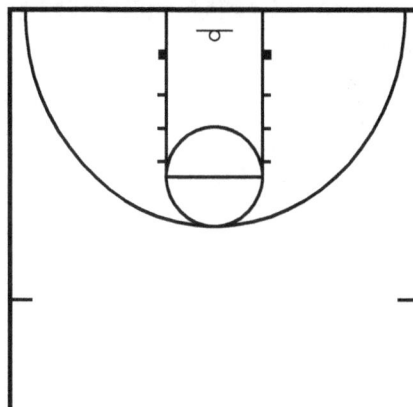

DO THEY LIKE TO RUN?   YES OR **NO**
WHERE DO THEY SHOOT FROM?   LEFT, RIGHT, OR **BOTH**
DO THEY ATTACK THE BASKET?   YES OR **NO**
DO THEY PRESS?   YES OR **NO**
IS MAN DEFENSE: TIGHT OR **SAGGING**

HOW DO THEY DEFEND THE POST? FORWARDS?

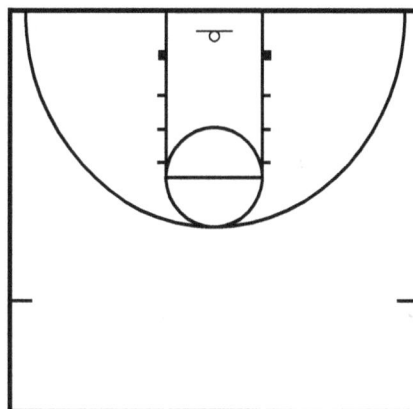

DEFENSIVE WEAK POINTS? PRESS WEAK POINTS?

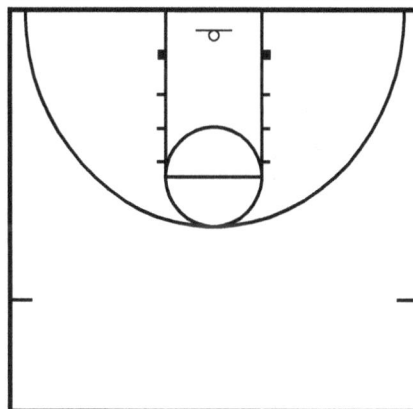

HOW DO WE COMBAT THEIR OFFENSIVE APPROACH?

HOW DO WE COMBAT THEIR DEFENSIVE APPROACH?

HOW WILL I DARE GREATLY? HOW WILL I IMPROVE ON MY 1% GOALS?

Film & Scouting

FILM &
SCOUTING REPORT

HOME:

GUEST:

DATE:

ASSIGNED COACH:

ASSIGNED PLAYER:

HOME

GUEST

SCORE:	1ST____	2ND____	3RD____	4TH____

MAN: Y OR N

ZONE SETS:

PRESS: Y OR N

DETAILS:

OFFENSE SETS:

SHOT CHART:

Q1

Q2

Q3

Q4

#	REBs	FLs	STs	TOs	#	REBs	FLs	STs	TOs

SCORE:	1ST____	2ND____	3RD____	4TH____

MAN: Y OR N

ZONE SETS:

PRESS: Y OR N

DETAILS:

OFFENSE SETS:

SHOT CHART:

Q1

Q2

Q3

Q4

#	REBs	FLs	STs	TOs	#	REBs	FLs	STs	TOs

Film & Scouting

FOR SCOUTING REPORTS:
WHO ARE THE KEY PERSONNEL TO KNOW OF? WHY?

WHAT ARE OUR LIKELY MATCHUPS?

DO THEY LIKE TO RUN?	YES or **NO**
WHERE DO THEY SHOOT FROM?	LEFT, RIGHT, or **BOTH**
DO THEY ATTACK THE BASKET?	YES or **NO**
DO THEY PRESS?	YES or **NO**
IS MAN DEFENSE:	TIGHT or **SAGGING**

HOW DO THEY DEFEND THE POST? FORWARDS?

DEFENSIVE WEAK POINTS? PRESS WEAK POINTS?

WHICH PLAYS SHOULD WE USE AGAINST THIS TEAM?

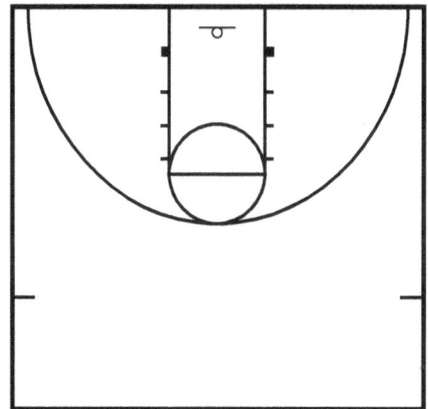

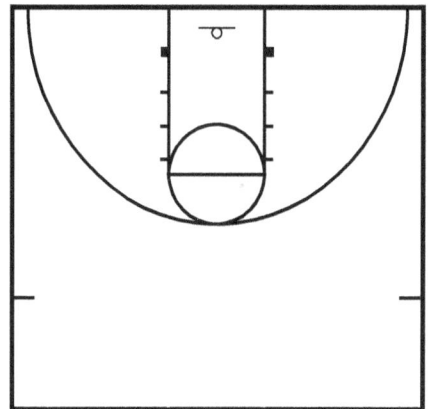

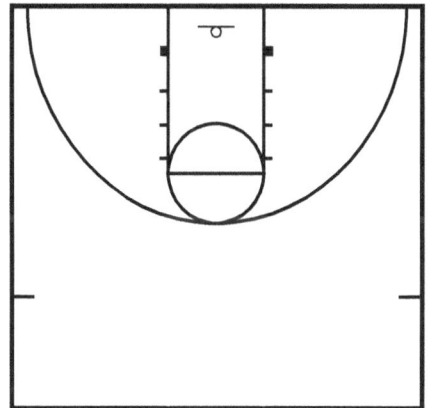

HOW DO WE COMBAT THEIR OFFENSIVE APPROACH?

HOW DO WE COMBAT THEIR DEFENSIVE APPROACH?

HOW WILL I DARE GREATLY? HOW WILL I IMPROVE ON MY 1% GOALS?

FILM &
SCOUTING REPORT

HOME:

GUEST:

DATE:

ASSIGNED COACH:

ASSIGNED PLAYER:

HOME

GUEST

SCORE:	1ST____	2ND____	3RD____	4TH____

MAN: Y OR N
ZONE SETS:

PRESS: Y OR N
DETAILS:

OFFENSE SETS:

SHOT CHART:

Q1

Q2

Q3

Q4

SCORE:	1ST____	2ND____	3RD____	4TH____

MAN: Y OR N
ZONE SETS:

PRESS: Y OR N
DETAILS:

OFFENSE SETS:

SHOT CHART:

Q1

Q2

Q3

Q4

#	REBs	FLs	STs	TOs	#	REBs	FLs	STs	TOs	#	REBs	FLs	STs	TOs	#	REBs	FLs	STs	TOs

Film & Scouting

FOR SCOUTING REPORTS:
WHO ARE THE KEY PERSONNEL TO KNOW OF? WHY?

WHAT ARE OUR LIKELY MATCHUPS?

DO THEY LIKE TO RUN?	YES or NO
WHERE DO THEY SHOOT FROM?	LEFT, RIGHT, or BOTH
DO THEY ATTACK THE BASKET?	YES or NO
DO THEY PRESS?	YES or NO
IS MAN DEFENSE:	TIGHT or SAGGING

HOW DO THEY DEFEND THE POST? FORWARDS?

DEFENSIVE WEAK POINTS? PRESS WEAK POINTS?

WHICH PLAYS SHOULD WE USE AGAINST THIS TEAM?

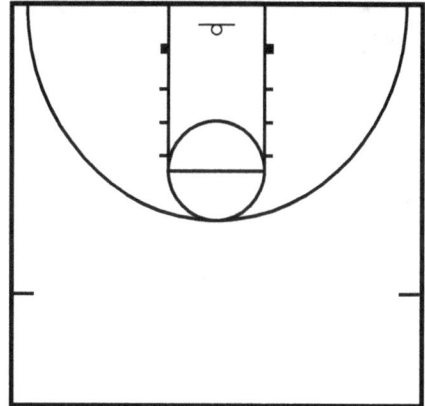

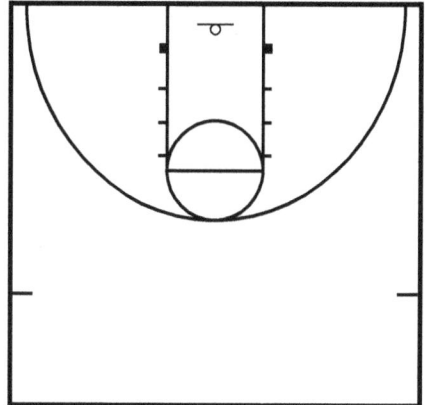

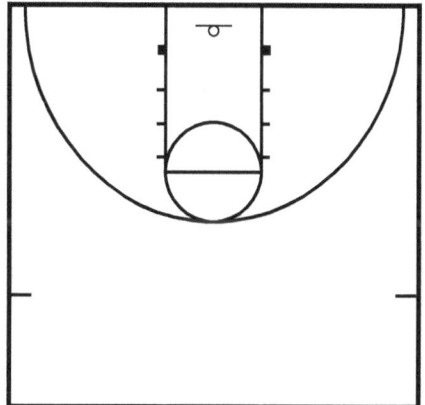

HOW DO WE COMBAT THEIR OFFENSIVE APPROACH?

HOW DO WE COMBAT THEIR DEFENSIVE APPROACH?

HOW WILL I DARE GREATLY? HOW WILL I IMPROVE ON MY 1% GOALS?

FILM & SCOUTING REPORT

HOME:

GUEST:

DATE:

ASSIGNED COACH:

ASSIGNED PLAYER:

HOME

GUEST

SCORE: 1ST____ 2ND____ 3RD____ 4TH____	**SCORE:** 1ST____ 2ND____ 3RD____ 4TH____

MAN: Y or N
ZONE SETS:

MAN: Y or N
ZONE SETS:

PRESS: Y or N
DETAILS:

PRESS: Y or N
DETAILS:

OFFENSE SETS:

OFFENSE SETS:

SHOT CHART:

Q1   Q2

Q3   Q4

SHOT CHART:

Q1   Q2

Q3   Q4

#	REBs	FLs	STs	TOs	#	REBs	FLs	STs	TOs	#	REBs	FLs	STs	TOs	#	REBs	FLs	STs	TOs

Film & Scouting

FOR SCOUTING REPORTS:
WHO ARE THE KEY PERSONNEL TO KNOW OF? WHY?

WHAT ARE OUR LIKELY MATCHUPS?

DO THEY LIKE TO RUN?	YES OR **NO**
WHERE DO THEY SHOOT FROM?	LEFT, RIGHT, OR **BOTH**
DO THEY ATTACK THE BASKET?	YES OR **NO**
DO THEY PRESS?	YES OR **NO**
IS MAN DEFENSE:	TIGHT OR **SAGGING**

HOW DO THEY DEFEND THE POST? FORWARDS?

DEFENSIVE WEAK POINTS? PRESS WEAK POINTS?

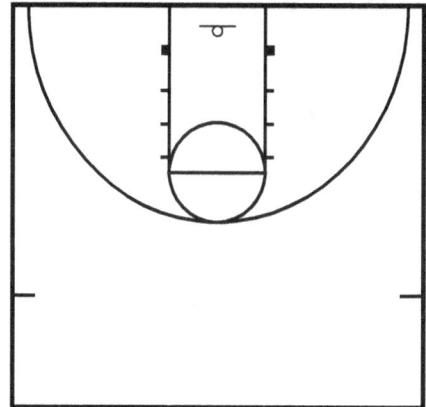

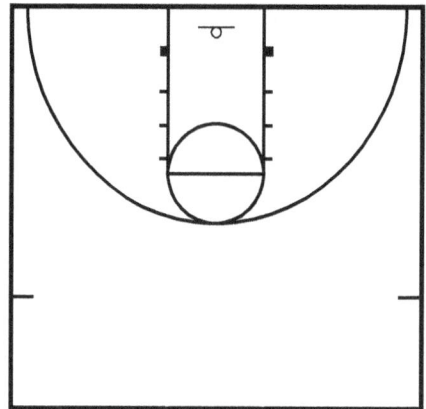

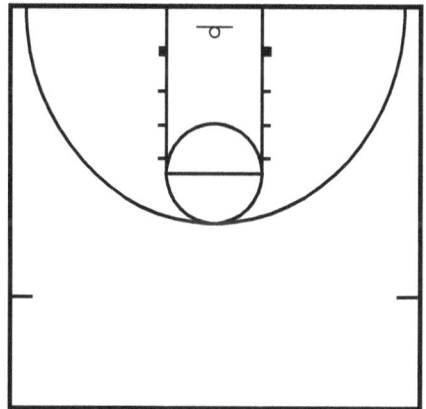

HOW DO WE COMBAT THEIR OFFENSIVE APPROACH?

HOW DO WE COMBAT THEIR DEFENSIVE APPROACH?

HOW WILL I DARE GREATLY? HOW WILL I IMPROVE ON MY 1% GOALS?

FILM & SCOUTING REPORT

HOME:

GUEST:

DATE:

ASSIGNED COACH:

ASSIGNED PLAYER:

HOME

SCORE: 1ST____ 2ND____ 3RD____ 4TH____

MAN: Y OR N
ZONE SETS:

PRESS: Y OR N
DETAILS:

OFFENSE SETS:

SHOT CHART:

Q1   Q2

Q3   Q4

#	REBs	FLs	STs	TOs	#	REBs	FLs	STs	TOs

GUEST

SCORE: 1ST____ 2ND____ 3RD____ 4TH____

MAN: Y OR N
ZONE SETS:

PRESS: Y OR N
DETAILS:

OFFENSE SETS:

SHOT CHART:

Q1   Q2

Q3   Q4

#	REBs	FLs	STs	TOs	#	REBs	FLs	STs	TOs

Film & Scouting

FOR SCOUTING REPORTS:
WHO ARE THE KEY PERSONNEL TO KNOW OF? WHY?

WHAT ARE OUR LIKELY MATCHUPS?

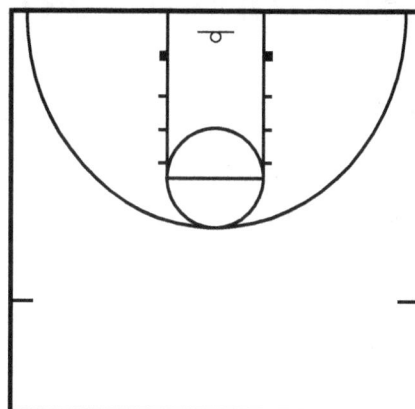

DO THEY LIKE TO RUN?   YES or NO
WHERE DO THEY SHOOT FROM?   LEFT, RIGHT, or BOTH
DO THEY ATTACK THE BASKET?   YES or NO
DO THEY PRESS?   YES or NO
IS MAN DEFENSE: TIGHT or SAGGING

HOW DO THEY DEFEND THE POST? FORWARDS?

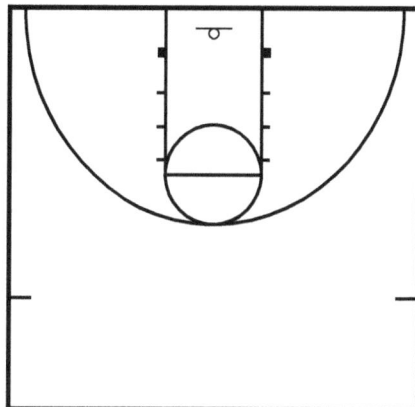

DEFENSIVE WEAK POINTS? PRESS WEAK POINTS?

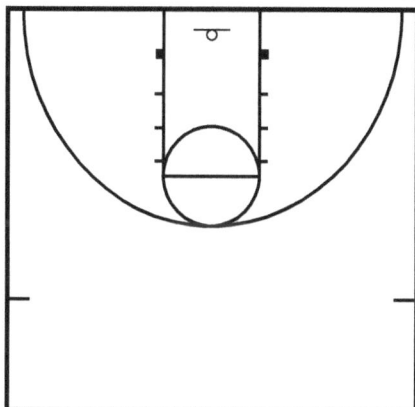

HOW DO WE COMBAT THEIR OFFENSIVE APPROACH?

HOW DO WE COMBAT THEIR DEFENSIVE APPROACH?

HOW WILL I DARE GREATLY? HOW WILL I IMPROVE ON MY 1% GOALS?

Film & Scouting

FILM &
SCOUTING REPORT

HOME:

GUEST:

DATE:

ASSIGNED COACH:

ASSIGNED PLAYER:

HOME

GUEST

	SCORE:	1ST_____	2ND_____	3RD_____	4TH_____

MAN: Y or N

ZONE SETS:

PRESS: Y or N

DETAILS:

OFFENSE SETS:

SHOT CHART:

Q1   Q2

Q3   Q4

	SCORE:	1ST_____	2ND_____	3RD_____	4TH_____

MAN: Y or N

ZONE SETS:

PRESS: Y or N

DETAILS:

OFFENSE SETS:

SHOT CHART:

Q1   Q2

Q3   Q4

#	REBs	FLs	STs	TOs	#	REBs	FLs	STs	TOs	#	REBs	FLs	STs	TOs	#	REBs	FLs	STs	TOs

Film & Scouting

FOR SCOUTING REPORTS:
WHO ARE THE KEY PERSONNEL TO KNOW OF? WHY?

WHAT ARE OUR LIKELY MATCHUPS?

DO THEY LIKE TO RUN?	YES or NO
WHERE DO THEY SHOOT FROM?	LEFT, RIGHT, or BOTH
DO THEY ATTACK THE BASKET?	YES or NO
DO THEY PRESS?	YES or NO
IS MAN DEFENSE:	TIGHT or SAGGING

HOW DO THEY DEFEND THE POST? FORWARDS?

DEFENSIVE WEAK POINTS? PRESS WEAK POINTS?

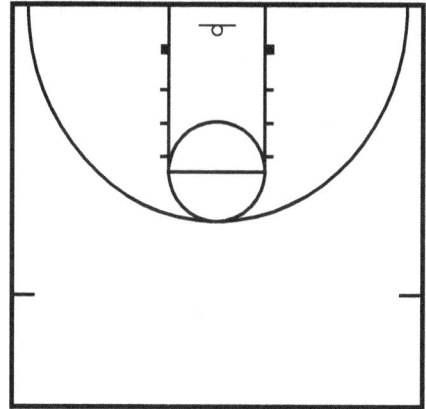

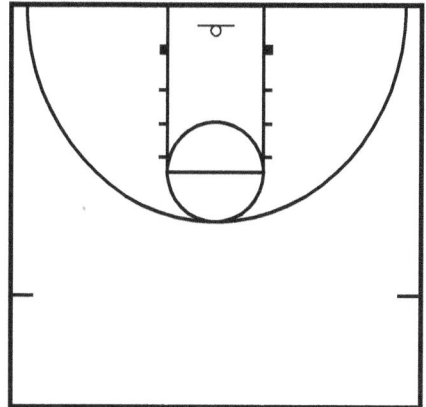

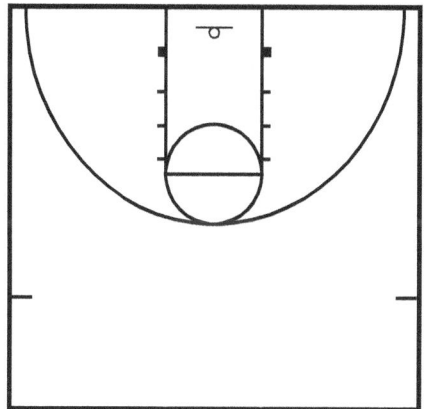

HOW DO WE COMBAT THEIR OFFENSIVE APPROACH?

HOW DO WE COMBAT THEIR DEFENSIVE APPROACH?

HOW WILL I DARE GREATLY? HOW WILL I IMPROVE ON MY 1% GOALS?

Film & Scouting

FILM & SCOUTING REPORT

HOME:

GUEST:

DATE:

ASSIGNED COACH:

ASSIGNED PLAYER:

HOME

GUEST

SCORE:	1ST_____ 2ND_____ 3RD_____ 4TH_____
MAN: ZONE SETS:	Y OR N
PRESS: DETAILS:	Y OR N

SCORE:	1ST_____ 2ND_____ 3RD_____ 4TH_____
MAN: ZONE SETS:	Y OR N
PRESS: DETAILS:	Y OR N

OFFENSE SETS:

OFFENSE SETS:

SHOT CHART:

Q1 Q2 Q3 Q4

SHOT CHART:

Q1 Q2 Q3 Q4

#	REBs	FLs	STs	TOs	#	REBs	FLs	STs	TOs

#	REBs	FLs	STs	TOs	#	REBs	FLs	STs	TOs

Film & Scouting

FOR SCOUTING REPORTS:
WHO ARE THE KEY PERSONNEL TO KNOW OF? WHY?

WHAT ARE OUR LIKELY MATCHUPS?

DO THEY LIKE TO RUN?	YES or NO
WHERE DO THEY SHOOT FROM?	LEFT, RIGHT, or BOTH
DO THEY ATTACK THE BASKET?	YES or NO
DO THEY PRESS?	YES or NO
IS MAN DEFENSE:	TIGHT or SAGGING

HOW DO THEY DEFEND THE POST? FORWARDS?

DEFENSIVE WEAK POINTS? PRESS WEAK POINTS?

WHICH PLAYS SHOULD WE USE AGAINST THIS TEAM?

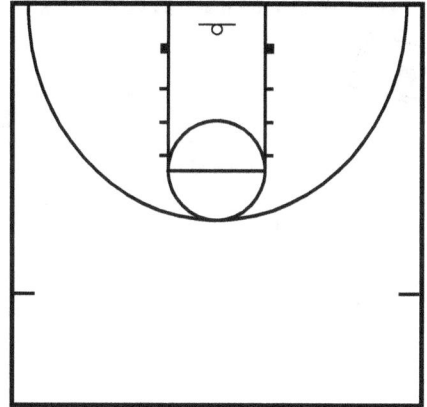

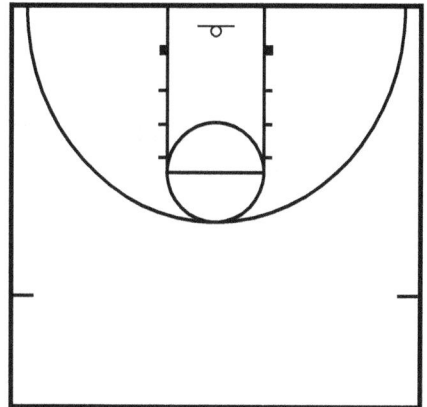

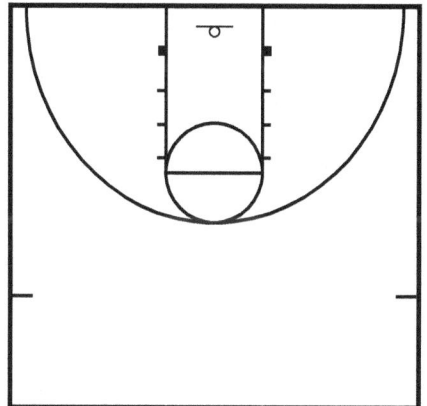

HOW DO WE COMBAT THEIR OFFENSIVE APPROACH?

HOW DO WE COMBAT THEIR DEFENSIVE APPROACH?

HOW WILL I DARE GREATLY? HOW WILL I IMPROVE ON MY 1% GOALS?

Film & Scouting

FILM & SCOUTING REPORT

HOME:

GUEST:

DATE:

ASSIGNED COACH:

ASSIGNED PLAYER:

HOME

GUEST

SCORE:	1ST____	2ND____	3RD____	4TH____

MAN: Y OR N

ZONE SETS:

PRESS: Y OR N

DETAILS:

OFFENSE SETS:

SHOT CHART:

Q1

Q2

Q3

Q4

#	REBs	FLs	STs	TOs	#	REBs	FLs	STs	TOs

SCORE:	1ST____	2ND____	3RD____	4TH____

MAN: Y OR N

ZONE SETS:

PRESS: Y OR N

DETAILS:

OFFENSE SETS:

SHOT CHART:

Q1

Q2

Q3

Q4

#	REBs	FLs	STs	TOs	#	REBs	FLs	STs	TOs

Film & Scouting

FOR SCOUTING REPORTS:
WHO ARE THE KEY PERSONNEL TO KNOW OF? WHY?

WHAT ARE OUR LIKELY MATCHUPS?

WHICH PLAYS SHOULD WE
USE AGAINST THIS TEAM?

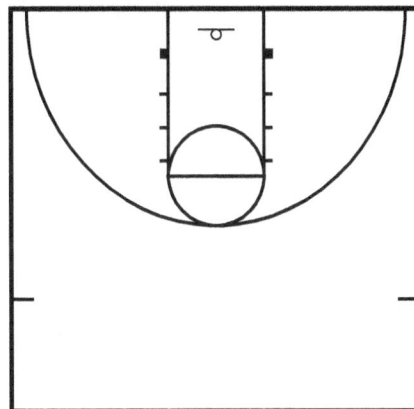

DO THEY LIKE TO RUN?	YES or NO
WHERE DO THEY SHOOT FROM?	LEFT, RIGHT, or BOTH
DO THEY ATTACK THE BASKET?	YES or NO
DO THEY PRESS?	YES or NO
IS MAN DEFENSE:	TIGHT or SAGGING

HOW DO THEY DEFEND THE POST? FORWARDS?

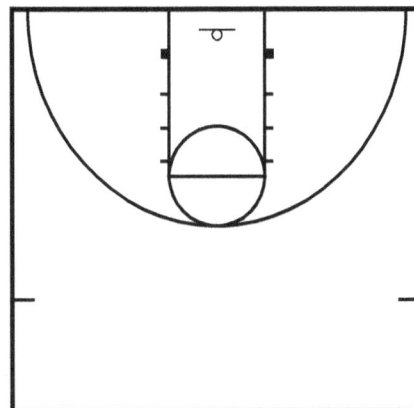

DEFENSIVE WEAK POINTS? PRESS WEAK POINTS?

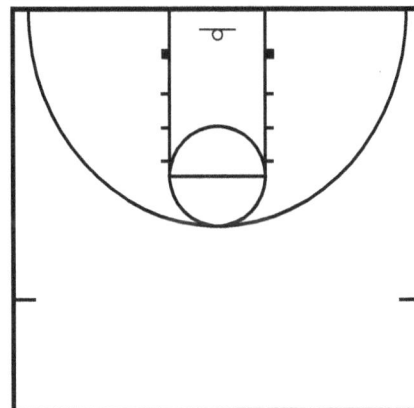

HOW DO WE COMBAT THEIR OFFENSIVE APPROACH?

HOW DO WE COMBAT THEIR DEFENSIVE APPROACH?

HOW WILL I DARE GREATLY? HOW WILL I IMPROVE ON MY 1% GOALS?

FILM &
SCOUTING REPORT

HOME:

GUEST:

DATE:

ASSIGNED COACH:

ASSIGNED PLAYER:

HOME

GUEST

	HOME					GUEST			
SCORE:	1ST___	2ND___	3RD___	4TH___	SCORE:	1ST___	2ND___	3RD___	4TH___

MAN: Y OR N
ZONE SETS:

PRESS: Y OR N
DETAILS:

OFFENSE SETS:

SHOT CHART:

Q1   Q2

Q3   Q4

MAN: Y OR N
ZONE SETS:

PRESS: Y OR N
DETAILS:

OFFENSE SETS:

SHOT CHART:

Q1   Q2

Q3   Q4

#	REBs	FLs	STs	TOs	#	REBs	FLs	STs	TOs	#	REBs	FLs	STs	TOs	#	REBs	FLs	STs	TOs

FOR SCOUTING REPORTS:
WHO ARE THE KEY PERSONNEL TO KNOW OF? WHY?

WHAT ARE OUR LIKELY MATCHUPS?

DO THEY LIKE TO RUN?	YES OR NO
WHERE DO THEY SHOOT FROM?	LEFT, RIGHT, OR BOTH
DO THEY ATTACK THE BASKET?	YES OR NO
DO THEY PRESS?	YES OR NO
IS MAN DEFENSE:	TIGHT OR SAGGING

HOW DO THEY DEFEND THE POST? FORWARDS?

DEFENSIVE WEAK POINTS? PRESS WEAK POINTS?

WHICH PLAYS SHOULD WE USE AGAINST THIS TEAM?

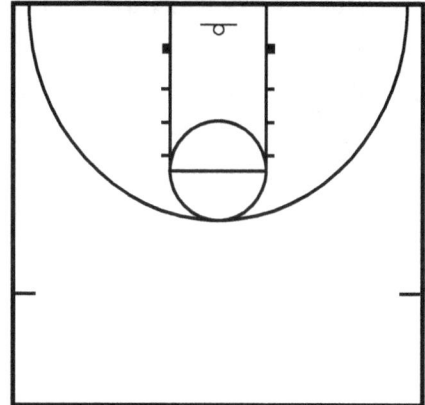

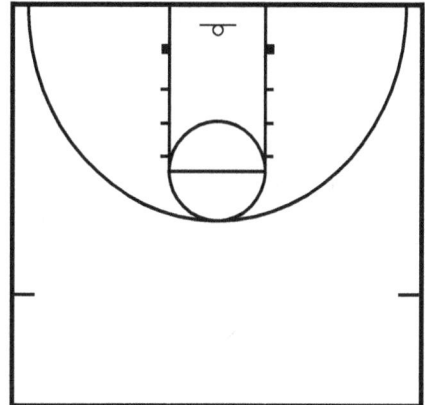

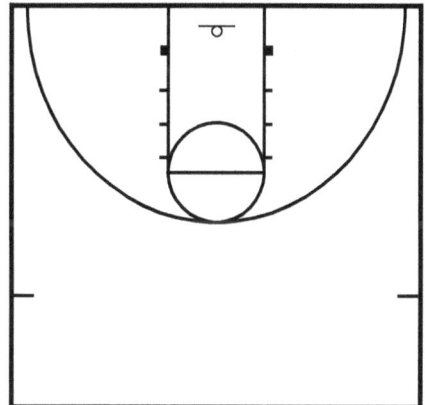

HOW DO WE COMBAT THEIR OFFENSIVE APPROACH?

HOW DO WE COMBAT THEIR DEFENSIVE APPROACH?

HOW WILL I DARE GREATLY? HOW WILL I IMPROVE ON MY 1% GOALS?

FILM &
SCOUTING REPORT

HOME:

GUEST:

DATE:

ASSIGNED COACH:

ASSIGNED PLAYER:

HOME

GUEST

	HOME		GUEST	
SCORE:	1ST____ 2ND____ 3RD____ 4TH____		SCORE:	1ST____ 2ND____ 3RD____ 4TH____

MAN: Y or N
ZONE SETS:

PRESS: Y or N
DETAILS:

MAN: Y or N
ZONE SETS:

PRESS: Y or N
DETAILS:

OFFENSE SETS:

OFFENSE SETS:

SHOT CHART:

Q1 Q2

Q3 Q4

SHOT CHART:

Q1 Q2

Q3 Q4

#	REBs	FLs	STs	TOs	#	REBs	FLs	STs	TOs	#	REBs	FLs	STs	TOs	#	REBs	FLs	STs	TOs

FOR SCOUTING REPORTS:
WHO ARE THE KEY PERSONNEL TO KNOW OF? WHY?

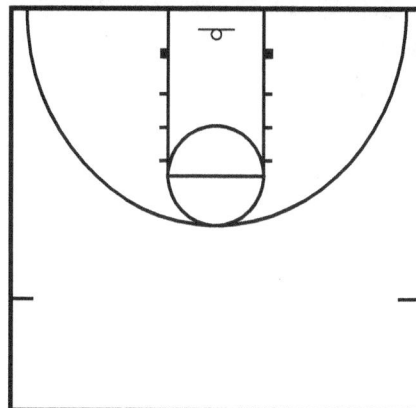

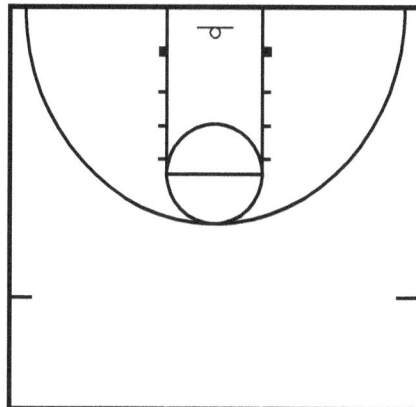

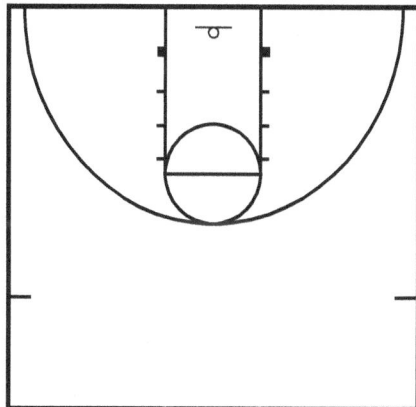

WHAT ARE OUR LIKELY MATCHUPS?

DO THEY LIKE TO RUN?	YES OR NO
WHERE DO THEY SHOOT FROM?	LEFT, RIGHT, OR BOTH
DO THEY ATTACK THE BASKET?	YES OR NO
DO THEY PRESS?	YES OR NO
IS MAN DEFENSE:	TIGHT OR SAGGING

HOW DO THEY DEFEND THE POST? FORWARDS?

DEFENSIVE WEAK POINTS? PRESS WEAK POINTS?

Film & Scouting

HOW DO WE COMBAT THEIR OFFENSIVE APPROACH?

HOW DO WE COMBAT THEIR DEFENSIVE APPROACH?

HOW WILL I DARE GREATLY? HOW WILL I IMPROVE ON MY 1% GOALS?

FILM &
SCOUTING REPORT

HOME:

GUEST:

DATE:

ASSIGNED COACH:

ASSIGNED PLAYER:

SCORE: | 1ST____ 2ND____ 3RD____ 4TH____

SCORE: | 1ST____ 2ND____ 3RD____ 4TH____

MAN:
ZONE SETS:

Y or N

PRESS:
DETAILS:

Y or N

MAN:
ZONE SETS:

Y or N

PRESS:
DETAILS:

Y or N

OFFENSE
SETS:

OFFENSE
SETS:

SHOT
CHART:

Q1

Q2

Q3

Q4

SHOT
CHART:

Q1

Q2

Q3

Q4

#	REBs	FLs	STs	TOs	#	REBs	FLs	STs	TOs	#	REBs	FLs	STs	TOs	#	REBs	FLs	STs	TOs

Film & Scouting

106

FOR SCOUTING REPORTS:
WHO ARE THE KEY PERSONNEL TO KNOW OF? WHY?

WHICH PLAYS SHOULD WE USE AGAINST THIS TEAM?

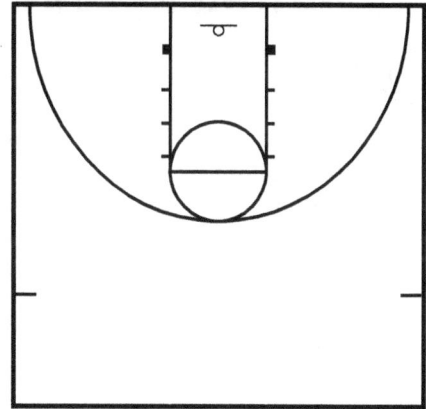

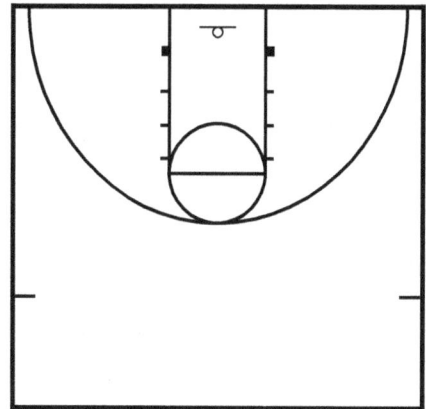

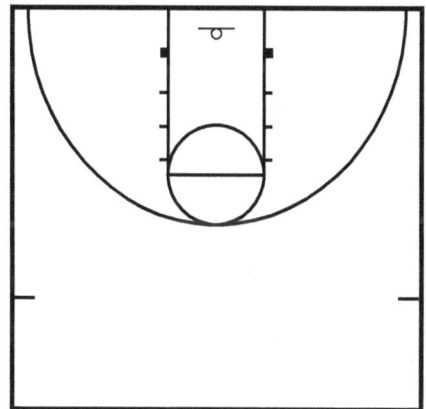

WHAT ARE OUR LIKELY MATCHUPS?

DO THEY LIKE TO RUN?	YES OR **NO**
WHERE DO THEY SHOOT FROM?	LEFT, RIGHT, OR **BOTH**
DO THEY ATTACK THE BASKET?	YES OR **NO**
DO THEY PRESS?	YES OR **NO**
IS MAN DEFENSE:	TIGHT OR **SAGGING**

HOW DO THEY DEFEND THE POST? FORWARDS?

DEFENSIVE WEAK POINTS? PRESS WEAK POINTS?

HOW DO WE COMBAT THEIR OFFENSIVE APPROACH?

HOW DO WE COMBAT THEIR DEFENSIVE APPROACH?

HOW WILL I DARE GREATLY? HOW WILL I IMPROVE ON MY 1% GOALS?

FILM & SCOUTING REPORT

HOME:

GUEST:

DATE:

ASSIGNED COACH:

ASSIGNED PLAYER:

HOME

GUEST

SCORE:	1ST____	2ND____	3RD____	4TH____

MAN: Y or N

ZONE SETS:

PRESS: Y or N

DETAILS:

OFFENSE SETS:

SHOT CHART:

Q1   Q2

Q3   Q4

SCORE:	1ST____	2ND____	3RD____	4TH____

MAN: Y or N

ZONE SETS:

PRESS: Y or N

DETAILS:

OFFENSE SETS:

SHOT CHART:

Q1   Q2

Q3   Q4

#	REBs	FLs	STs	TOs	#	REBs	FLs	STs	TOs

#	REBs	FLs	STs	TOs	#	REBs	FLs	STs	TOs

FOR SCOUTING REPORTS:
WHO ARE THE KEY PERSONNEL TO KNOW OF? WHY?

WHAT ARE OUR LIKELY MATCHUPS?

DO THEY LIKE TO RUN?	YES OR **NO**
WHERE DO THEY SHOOT FROM?	LEFT, RIGHT, OR **BOTH**
DO THEY ATTACK THE BASKET?	YES OR **NO**
DO THEY PRESS?	YES OR **NO**
IS MAN DEFENSE:	TIGHT OR **SAGGING**

HOW DO THEY DEFEND THE POST? FORWARDS?

DEFENSIVE WEAK POINTS? PRESS WEAK POINTS?

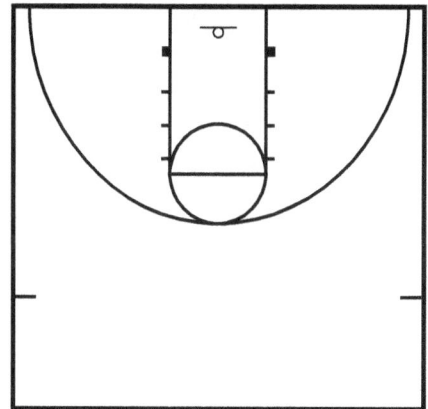

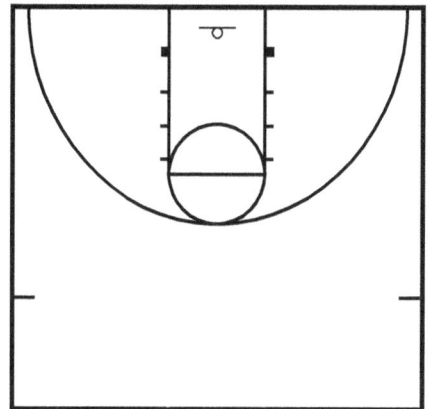

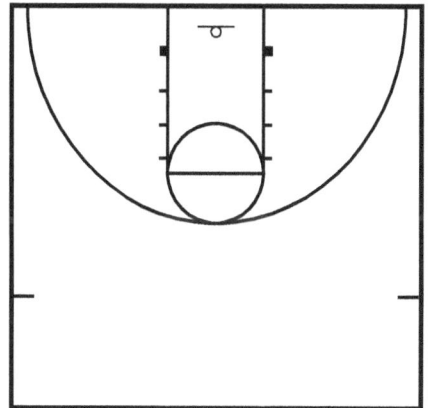

HOW DO WE COMBAT THEIR OFFENSIVE APPROACH?

HOW DO WE COMBAT THEIR DEFENSIVE APPROACH?

HOW WILL I DARE GREATLY? HOW WILL I IMPROVE ON MY 1% GOALS?

Film & Scouting

FILM &
SCOUTING REPORT

HOME:

GUEST:

DATE:

ASSIGNED COACH:

ASSIGNED PLAYER:

HOME

GUEST

	HOME		GUEST	
SCORE:	1ST___ 2ND___ 3RD___ 4TH___		1ST___ 2ND___ 3RD___ 4TH___	

MAN: Y or N
ZONE SETS:

PRESS: Y or N
DETAILS:

OFFENSE SETS:

SHOT CHART:

Q1   Q2

Q3   Q4

MAN: Y or N
ZONE SETS:

PRESS: Y or N
DETAILS:

OFFENSE SETS:

SHOT CHART:

Q1   Q2

Q3   Q4

#	REBs	FLs	STs	TOs	#	REBs	FLs	STs	TOs

#	REBs	FLs	STs	TOs	#	REBs	FLs	STs	TOs

FOR SCOUTING REPORTS:
WHO ARE THE KEY PERSONNEL TO KNOW OF? WHY?

WHAT ARE OUR LIKELY MATCHUPS?

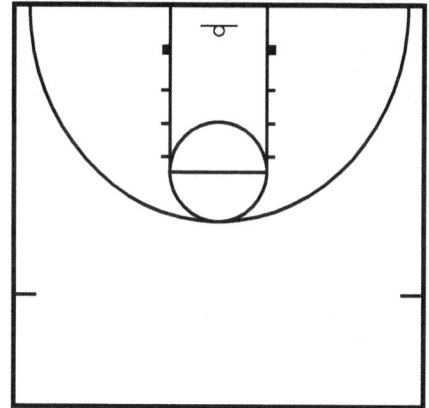

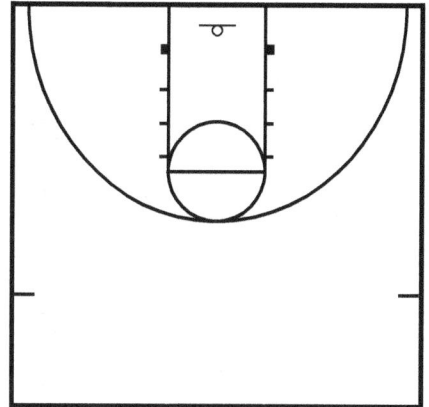

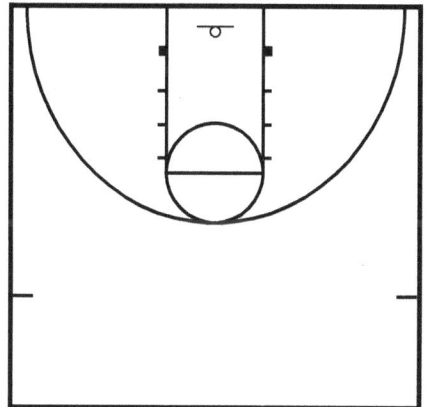

DO THEY LIKE TO RUN?	**YES** OR **NO**
WHERE DO THEY SHOOT FROM?	**LEFT, RIGHT,** OR **BOTH**
DO THEY ATTACK THE BASKET?	**YES** OR **NO**
DO THEY PRESS?	**YES** OR **NO**
IS MAN DEFENSE:	**TIGHT** OR **SAGGING**

HOW DO THEY DEFEND THE POST? FORWARDS?

DEFENSIVE WEAK POINTS? PRESS WEAK POINTS?

HOW DO WE COMBAT THEIR OFFENSIVE APPROACH?

HOW DO WE COMBAT THEIR DEFENSIVE APPROACH?

HOW WILL I DARE GREATLY? HOW WILL I IMPROVE ON MY 1% GOALS?

FILM & SCOUTING REPORT

HOME: _____

GUEST: _____

DATE: _____

ASSIGNED COACH: _____

ASSIGNED PLAYER: _____

HOME

SCORE: 1ST_____ 2ND_____ 3RD_____ 4TH_____

MAN: Y or N

ZONE SETS:

PRESS: Y or N

DETAILS:

OFFENSE SETS:

SHOT CHART:

Q1

Q2

Q3

Q4

#	REBs	FLs	STs	TOs	#	REBs	FLs	STs	TOs

GUEST

SCORE: 1ST_____ 2ND_____ 3RD_____ 4TH_____

MAN: Y or N

ZONE SETS:

PRESS: Y or N

DETAILS:

OFFENSE SETS:

SHOT CHART:

Q1

Q2

Q3

Q4

#	REBs	FLs	STs	TOs	#	REBs	FLs	STs	TOs

Film & Scouting

FOR SCOUTING REPORTS:
WHO ARE THE KEY PERSONNEL TO KNOW OF? WHY?

WHICH PLAYS SHOULD WE USE AGAINST THIS TEAM?

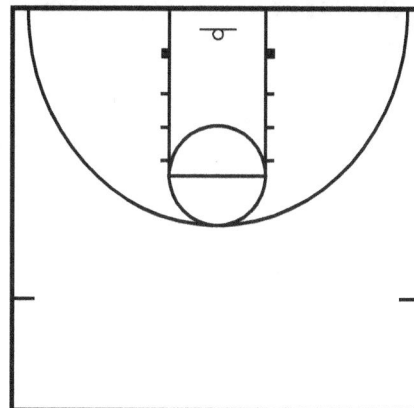

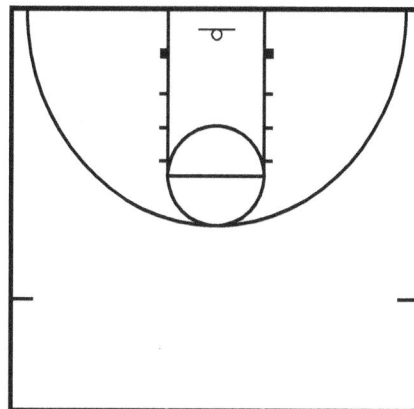

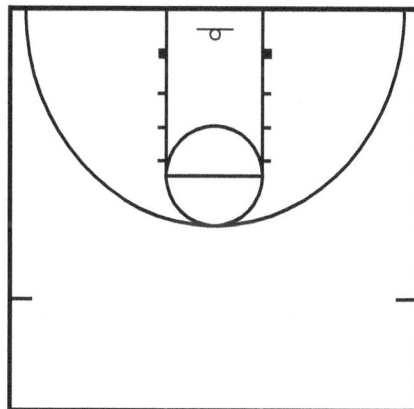

WHAT ARE OUR LIKELY MATCHUPS?

DO THEY LIKE TO RUN?	**YES** OR **NO**
WHERE DO THEY SHOOT FROM?	**LEFT, RIGHT,** OR **BOTH**
DO THEY ATTACK THE BASKET?	**YES** OR **NO**
DO THEY PRESS?	**YES** OR **NO**
IS MAN DEFENSE:	**TIGHT** OR **SAGGING**

HOW DO THEY DEFEND THE POST? FORWARDS?

DEFENSIVE WEAK POINTS? PRESS WEAK POINTS?

HOW DO WE COMBAT THEIR OFFENSIVE APPROACH?

HOW DO WE COMBAT THEIR DEFENSIVE APPROACH?

HOW WILL I DARE GREATLY? HOW WILL I IMPROVE ON MY 1% GOALS?

FILM &
SCOUTING REPORT

HOME: _____

GUEST: _____

DATE: _____

ASSIGNED COACH: _____

ASSIGNED PLAYER: _____

HOME

GUEST

SCORE:	1ST____	2ND____	3RD____	4TH____

MAN: **Y** OR **N**

ZONE SETS:

PRESS: **Y** OR **N**

DETAILS:

OFFENSE SETS:

SHOT CHART:

Q1　　Q2

Q3　　Q4

SCORE:	1ST____	2ND____	3RD____	4TH____

MAN: **Y** OR **N**

ZONE SETS:

PRESS: **Y** OR **N**

DETAILS:

OFFENSE SETS:

SHOT CHART:

Q1　　Q2

Q3　　Q4

#	REBs	FLs	STs	TOs	#	REBs	FLs	STs	TOs

#	REBs	FLs	STs	TOs	#	REBs	FLs	STs	TOs

Film & Scouting

FOR SCOUTING REPORTS:
WHO ARE THE KEY PERSONNEL TO KNOW OF? WHY?

WHAT ARE OUR LIKELY MATCHUPS?

DO THEY LIKE TO RUN?	YES or NO
WHERE DO THEY SHOOT FROM?	LEFT, RIGHT, or BOTH
DO THEY ATTACK THE BASKET?	YES or NO
DO THEY PRESS?	YES or NO
IS MAN DEFENSE:	TIGHT or SAGGING

HOW DO THEY DEFEND THE POST? FORWARDS?

DEFENSIVE WEAK POINTS? PRESS WEAK POINTS?

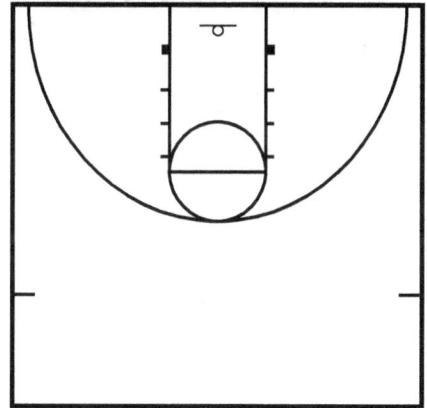

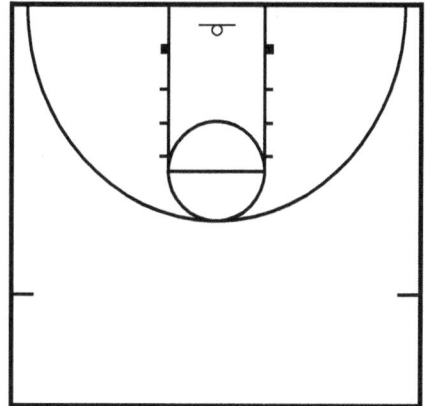

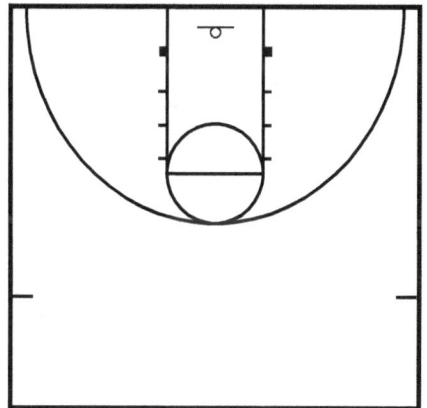

WHICH PLAYS SHOULD WE USE AGAINST THIS TEAM?

HOW DO WE COMBAT THEIR OFFENSIVE APPROACH?

HOW DO WE COMBAT THEIR DEFENSIVE APPROACH?

HOW WILL I DARE GREATLY? HOW WILL I IMPROVE ON MY 1% GOALS?

Film & Scouting

FILM & SCOUTING REPORT

HOME: _____ DATE: _____ ASSIGNED COACH: _____

GUEST: _____ ASSIGNED PLAYER: _____

HOME

GUEST

SCORE:	1ST____ 2ND____ 3RD____ 4TH____	SCORE:	1ST____ 2ND____ 3RD____ 4TH____

MAN: Y or N
ZONE SETS:

PRESS: Y or N
DETAILS:

MAN: Y or N
ZONE SETS:

PRESS: Y or N
DETAILS:

OFFENSE SETS:

OFFENSE SETS:

SHOT CHART:

Q1   Q2
Q3   Q4

SHOT CHART:

Q1   Q2
Q3   Q4

#	REBs	FLs	STs	TOs	#	REBs	FLs	STs	TOs

#	REBs	FLs	STs	TOs	#	REBs	FLs	STs	TOs

Film & Scouting

FOR SCOUTING REPORTS:
  WHO ARE THE KEY PERSONNEL TO KNOW OF? WHY?

WHICH PLAYS SHOULD WE USE AGAINST THIS TEAM?

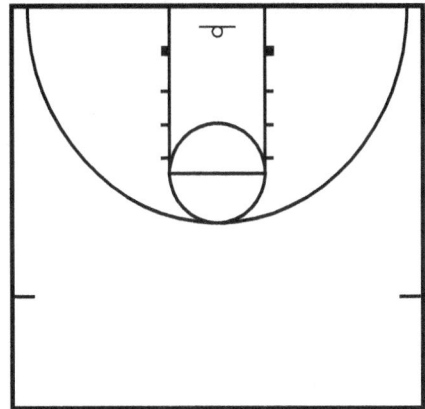

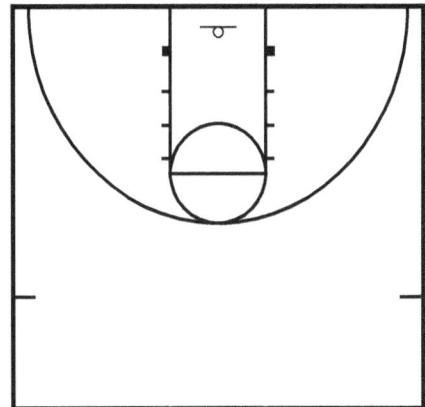

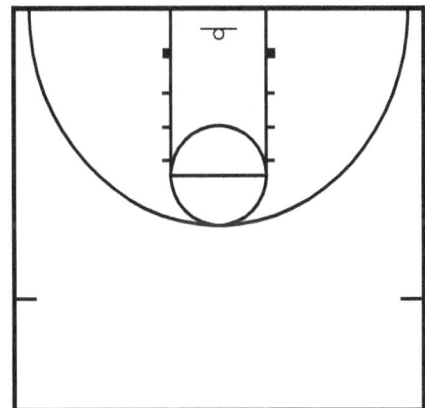

WHAT ARE OUR LIKELY MATCHUPS?

DO THEY LIKE TO RUN?	YES or NO
WHERE DO THEY SHOOT FROM?	LEFT, RIGHT, or BOTH
DO THEY ATTACK THE BASKET?	YES or NO
DO THEY PRESS?	YES or NO
IS MAN DEFENSE:	TIGHT or SAGGING

HOW DO THEY DEFEND THE POST? FORWARDS?

DEFENSIVE WEAK POINTS? PRESS WEAK POINTS?

HOW DO WE COMBAT THEIR OFFENSIVE APPROACH?

HOW DO WE COMBAT THEIR DEFENSIVE APPROACH?

HOW WILL I DARE GREATLY? HOW WILL I IMPROVE ON MY 1% GOALS?

FILM & SCOUTING REPORT

HOME:

GUEST:

DATE:

ASSIGNED COACH:

ASSIGNED PLAYER:

	HOME		GUEST	
SCORE:	1ST____ 2ND____ 3RD____ 4TH____		**SCORE:**	1ST____ 2ND____ 3RD____ 4TH____

MAN: Y or N
ZONE SETS:

PRESS: Y or N
DETAILS:

OFFENSE SETS:

SHOT CHART:

Q1   Q2

Q3   Q4

MAN: Y or N
ZONE SETS:

PRESS: Y or N
DETAILS:

OFFENSE SETS:

SHOT CHART:

Q1   Q2

Q3   Q4

#	REBs	FLs	STs	TOs	#	REBs	FLs	STs	TOs	#	REBs	FLs	STs	TOs	#	REBs	FLs	STs	TOs

Film & Scouting

FOR SCOUTING REPORTS:
WHO ARE THE KEY PERSONNEL TO KNOW OF? WHY?

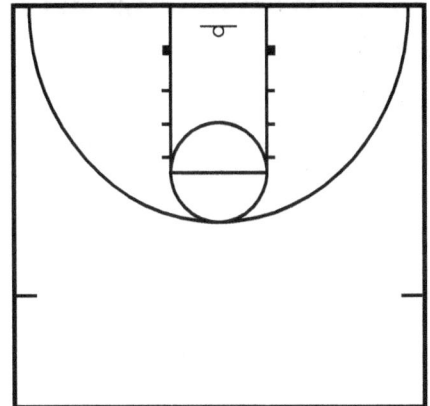

WHAT ARE OUR LIKELY MATCHUPS?

DO THEY LIKE TO RUN?	YES OR **NO**
WHERE DO THEY SHOOT FROM?	LEFT, RIGHT, OR **BOTH**
DO THEY ATTACK THE BASKET?	YES OR **NO**
DO THEY PRESS?	YES OR **NO**
IS MAN DEFENSE:	TIGHT OR **SAGGING**

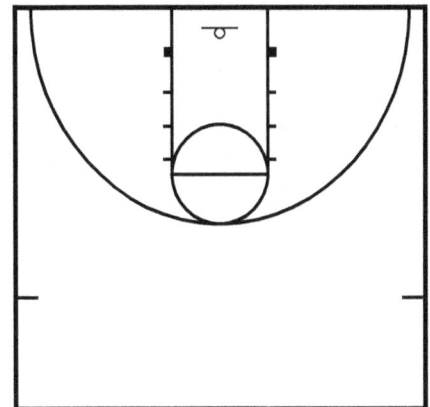

HOW DO THEY DEFEND THE POST? FORWARDS?

DEFENSIVE WEAK POINTS? PRESS WEAK POINTS?

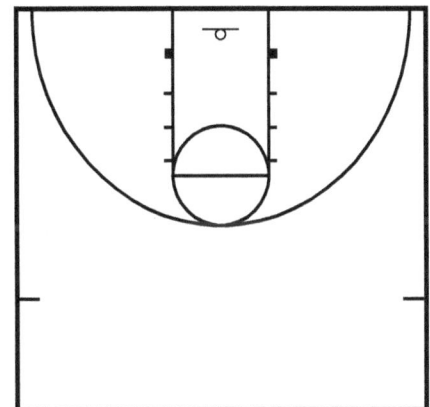

HOW DO WE COMBAT THEIR OFFENSIVE APPROACH?

HOW DO WE COMBAT THEIR DEFENSIVE APPROACH?

HOW WILL I DARE GREATLY? HOW WILL I IMPROVE ON MY 1% GOALS?

Film & Scouting

FILM &
SCOUTING REPORT

HOME:

GUEST:

DATE:

ASSIGNED COACH:

ASSIGNED PLAYER:

HOME

GUEST

SCORE:	1ST____ 2ND____ 3RD____ 4TH____		

MAN: Y or N

ZONE SETS:

PRESS: Y or N

DETAILS:

OFFENSE SETS:

SHOT CHART:

Q1

Q2

Q3

Q4

SCORE:	1ST____ 2ND____ 3RD____ 4TH____

MAN: Y or N

ZONE SETS:

PRESS: Y or N

DETAILS:

OFFENSE SETS:

SHOT CHART:

Q1

Q2

Q3

Q4

#	REBs	FLs	STs	TOs	#	REBs	FLs	STs	TOs

#	REBs	FLs	STs	TOs	#	REBs	FLs	STs	TOs

FOR SCOUTING REPORTS:
WHO ARE THE KEY PERSONNEL TO KNOW OF? WHY?

WHAT ARE OUR LIKELY MATCHUPS?

DO THEY LIKE TO RUN?	YES or **NO**
WHERE DO THEY SHOOT FROM?	**LEFT, RIGHT,** or **BOTH**
DO THEY ATTACK THE BASKET?	YES or **NO**
DO THEY PRESS?	YES or **NO**
IS MAN DEFENSE:	**TIGHT** or **SAGGING**

HOW DO THEY DEFEND THE POST? FORWARDS?

DEFENSIVE WEAK POINTS? PRESS WEAK POINTS?

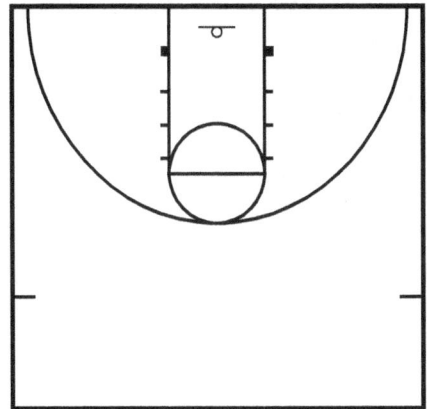

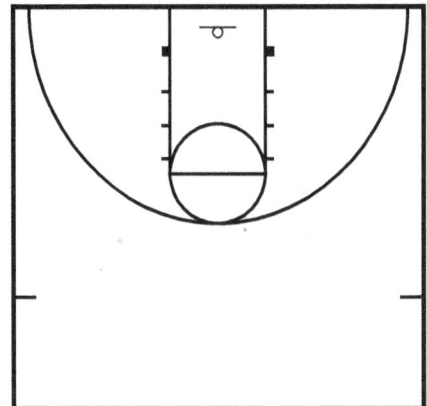

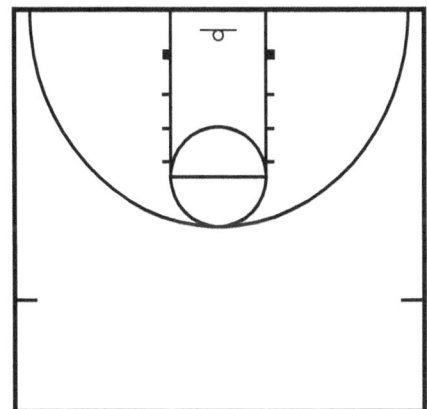

HOW DO WE COMBAT THEIR OFFENSIVE APPROACH?

HOW DO WE COMBAT THEIR DEFENSIVE APPROACH?

HOW WILL I DARE GREATLY? HOW WILL I IMPROVE ON MY 1% GOALS?

Film & Scouting

FILM & SCOUTING REPORT

HOME:

GUEST:

DATE:

ASSIGNED COACH:

ASSIGNED PLAYER:

HOME
GUEST

	HOME					GUEST			
SCORE:	1ST____	2ND____	3RD____	4TH____	**SCORE:**	1ST____	2ND____	3RD____	4TH____

MAN: Y or N
ZONE SETS:

PRESS: Y or N
DETAILS:

MAN: Y or N
ZONE SETS:

PRESS: Y or N
DETAILS:

OFFENSE SETS:

OFFENSE SETS:

SHOT CHART:

Q1   Q2

Q3   Q4

SHOT CHART:

Q1   Q2

Q3   Q4

#	REBs	FLs	STs	TOs	#	REBs	FLs	STs	TOs	#	REBs	FLs	STs	TOs	#	REBs	FLs	STs	TOs

Film & Scouting

FOR SCOUTING REPORTS:
WHO ARE THE KEY PERSONNEL TO KNOW OF? WHY?

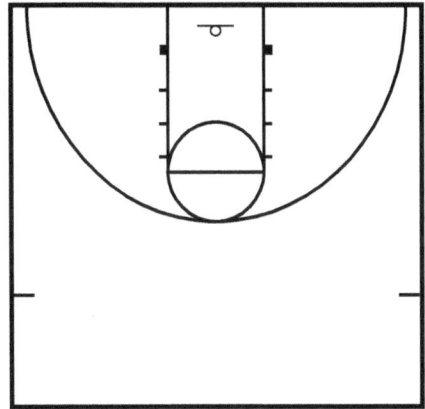

WHAT ARE OUR LIKELY MATCHUPS?

DO THEY LIKE TO RUN?	YES OR **NO**
WHERE DO THEY SHOOT FROM?	LEFT, RIGHT, OR **BOTH**
DO THEY ATTACK THE BASKET?	YES OR **NO**
DO THEY PRESS?	YES OR **NO**
IS MAN DEFENSE:	TIGHT OR **SAGGING**

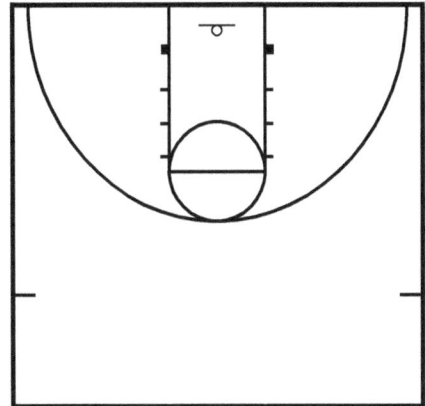

HOW DO THEY DEFEND THE POST? FORWARDS?

DEFENSIVE WEAK POINTS? PRESS WEAK POINTS?

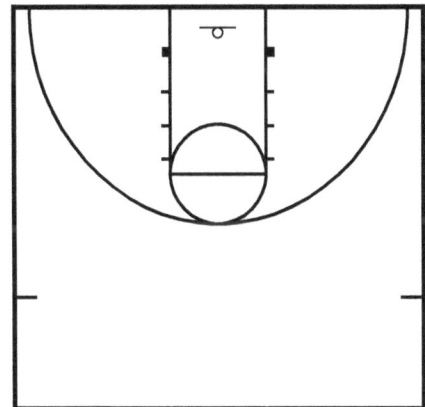

HOW DO WE COMBAT THEIR OFFENSIVE APPROACH?

HOW DO WE COMBAT THEIR DEFENSIVE APPROACH?

HOW WILL I DARE GREATLY? HOW WILL I IMPROVE ON MY 1% GOALS?

Film & Scouting

Post-Game Reviews

GAME #1
POST-GAME REVIEW

VERSUS:

WIN or LOSS   FINAL SCORE: _____ _____

HOME or AWAY | DATE/TIME:

OVERALL ASSESSMENT

DID WE DARE GREATLY?   YES or NO

HOW DID OUR PERSONNEL PLAY?

OFFENSIVELY, WHAT DO WE IMPROVE?

OVERALL, WHAT WENT RIGHT?

DEFENSIVELY, WHAT DO WE IMPROVE?

OVERALL, WHAT WENT WRONG?

DID I DARE GREATLY? HOW?

GAME #2
POST-GAME REVIEW

VERSUS:

HOME OR AWAY **DATE/TIME:**

WIN OR LOSS **FINAL SCORE:** _____ _____

OVERALL ASSESSMENT

DID WE DARE GREATLY? **YES OR NO**

HOW DID OUR PERSONNEL PLAY?

OFFENSIVELY, WHAT DO WE IMPROVE?

OVERALL, WHAT WENT RIGHT?

DEFENSIVELY, WHAT DO WE IMPROVE?

OVERALL, WHAT WENT WRONG?

DID I DARE GREATLY? HOW?

GAME #3
POST-GAME REVIEW

VERSUS:

HOME or AWAY | DATE/TIME:

WIN or LOSS   FINAL SCORE: _____ _____

OVERALL ASSESSMENT

DID WE DARE GREATLY?   YES or NO

HOW DID OUR PERSONNEL PLAY?

OFFENSIVELY, WHAT DO WE IMPROVE?

OVERALL, WHAT WENT RIGHT?

DEFENSIVELY, WHAT DO WE IMPROVE?

OVERALL, WHAT WENT WRONG?

DID I DARE GREATLY? HOW?

GAME #4
POST-GAME REVIEW

VERSUS:

HOME OR AWAY

DATE/TIME:

WIN OR LOSS   FINAL SCORE: _____ _____

OVERALL ASSESSMENT

DID WE DARE GREATLY?   YES OR NO

HOW DID OUR PERSONNEL PLAY?

OFFENSIVELY, WHAT DO WE IMPROVE?

OVERALL, WHAT WENT RIGHT?

DEFENSIVELY, WHAT DO WE IMPROVE?

OVERALL, WHAT WENT WRONG?

DID I DARE GREATLY? HOW?

GAME #5
POST-GAME REVIEW

VERSUS:

HOME OR AWAY | DATE/TIME:

WIN OR LOSS   FINAL SCORE: _____ _____

OVERALL ASSESSMENT

DID WE DARE GREATLY?   YES OR NO

HOW DID OUR PERSONNEL PLAY?

OFFENSIVELY, WHAT DO WE IMPROVE?

OVERALL, WHAT WENT RIGHT?

DEFENSIVELY, WHAT DO WE IMPROVE?

OVERALL, WHAT WENT WRONG?

DID I DARE GREATLY? HOW?

GAME #6
POST-GAME REVIEW

VERSUS:

HOME or AWAY

DATE/TIME:

WIN or LOSS   FINAL SCORE: _____ _____

OVERALL ASSESSMENT

DID WE DARE GREATLY?   YES or NO

HOW DID OUR PERSONNEL PLAY?

OFFENSIVELY, WHAT DO WE IMPROVE?

OVERALL, WHAT WENT RIGHT?

DEFENSIVELY, WHAT DO WE IMPROVE?

OVERALL, WHAT WENT WRONG?

DID I DARE GREATLY? HOW?

GAME #7
POST-GAME REVIEW

VERSUS:

HOME or AWAY   DATE/TIME:

WIN or LOSS   FINAL SCORE: _____ _____

**OVERALL
ASSESSMENT**

DID WE
DARE GREATLY?   YES or NO

HOW DID OUR PERSONNEL PLAY?

OFFENSIVELY, WHAT DO WE IMPROVE?

OVERALL, WHAT WENT RIGHT?

DEFENSIVELY, WHAT DO WE IMPROVE?

OVERALL, WHAT WENT WRONG?

DID I DARE GREATLY? HOW?

GAME #8
POST-GAME REVIEW

VERSUS:

HOME OR **AWAY**   **DATE/TIME:**

WIN OR **LOSS**   **FINAL SCORE:** _____ _____

**OVERALL
ASSESSMENT**

**DID WE
DARE GREATLY?**   **YES** OR **NO**

HOW DID OUR PERSONNEL PLAY?

OFFENSIVELY, WHAT DO WE IMPROVE?

OVERALL, WHAT WENT RIGHT?

DEFENSIVELY, WHAT DO WE IMPROVE?

OVERALL, WHAT WENT WRONG?

DID I DARE GREATLY? HOW?

GAME #9
POST-GAME REVIEW

VERSUS:

HOME or AWAY

DATE/TIME:

WIN or LOSS   FINAL SCORE: _____ _____

**OVERALL
ASSESSMENT**

**DID WE
DARE GREATLY?**   YES or NO

HOW DID OUR PERSONNEL PLAY?

OFFENSIVELY, WHAT DO WE IMPROVE?

OVERALL, WHAT WENT RIGHT?

DEFENSIVELY, WHAT DO WE IMPROVE?

OVERALL, WHAT WENT WRONG?

DID I DARE GREATLY? HOW?

GAME #10
POST-GAME REVIEW

VERSUS:

HOME OR AWAY | **DATE/TIME:**

WIN OR LOSS   **FINAL SCORE:** _____ _____

OVERALL ASSESSMENT

DID WE DARE GREATLY?   **YES OR NO**

HOW DID OUR PERSONNEL PLAY?

OFFENSIVELY, WHAT DO WE IMPROVE?

OVERALL, WHAT WENT RIGHT?

DEFENSIVELY, WHAT DO WE IMPROVE?

OVERALL, WHAT WENT WRONG?

DID I DARE GREATLY? HOW?

GAME #11
POST-GAME REVIEW

VERSUS:

HOME or AWAY   DATE/TIME:

WIN or LOSS   FINAL SCORE: _____ _____

**OVERALL
ASSESSMENT**

**DID WE
DARE GREATLY?**   YES or NO

HOW DID OUR PERSONNEL PLAY?

OFFENSIVELY, WHAT DO WE IMPROVE?

OVERALL, WHAT WENT RIGHT?

DEFENSIVELY, WHAT DO WE IMPROVE?

OVERALL, WHAT WENT WRONG?

DID I DARE GREATLY? HOW?

GAME #12
POST-GAME REVIEW

VERSUS: _____

HOME OR AWAY

DATE/TIME:

WIN OR LOSS

FINAL SCORE: _____ _____

OVERALL ASSESSMENT

DID WE DARE GREATLY? YES OR NO

HOW DID OUR PERSONNEL PLAY?

OFFENSIVELY, WHAT DO WE IMPROVE?

OVERALL, WHAT WENT RIGHT?

DEFENSIVELY, WHAT DO WE IMPROVE?

OVERALL, WHAT WENT WRONG?

DID I DARE GREATLY? HOW?

GAME #13
POST-GAME REVIEW

VERSUS:

WIN or LOSS   FINAL SCORE: _____ _____

HOME or AWAY | DATE/TIME:

OVERALL ASSESSMENT

DID WE DARE GREATLY?   YES or NO

HOW DID OUR PERSONNEL PLAY?

OFFENSIVELY, WHAT DO WE IMPROVE?

OVERALL, WHAT WENT RIGHT?

DEFENSIVELY, WHAT DO WE IMPROVE?

OVERALL, WHAT WENT WRONG?

DID I DARE GREATLY? HOW?

GAME #14
POST-GAME REVIEW

VERSUS:

HOME or AWAY DATE/TIME:

WIN or LOSS   FINAL SCORE: _____ _____

OVERALL ASSESSMENT

DID WE DARE GREATLY? YES or NO

HOW DID OUR PERSONNEL PLAY?

OFFENSIVELY, WHAT DO WE IMPROVE?

OVERALL, WHAT WENT RIGHT?

DEFENSIVELY, WHAT DO WE IMPROVE?

OVERALL, WHAT WENT WRONG?

DID I DARE GREATLY? HOW?

GAME #15
POST-GAME REVIEW

VERSUS:

HOME or AWAY | DATE/TIME:

WIN or LOSS   FINAL SCORE: _____ _____

OVERALL ASSESSMENT

DID WE DARE GREATLY?   YES or NO

HOW DID OUR PERSONNEL PLAY?

OFFENSIVELY, WHAT DO WE IMPROVE?

OVERALL, WHAT WENT RIGHT?

DEFENSIVELY, WHAT DO WE IMPROVE?

OVERALL, WHAT WENT WRONG?

DID I DARE GREATLY? HOW?

GAME #16
POST-GAME REVIEW

VERSUS:

HOME OR AWAY | DATE/TIME:

WIN OR LOSS   FINAL SCORE: _____ _____

OVERALL ASSESSMENT

DID WE DARE GREATLY? YES OR NO

HOW DID OUR PERSONNEL PLAY?

OFFENSIVELY, WHAT DO WE IMPROVE?

OVERALL, WHAT WENT RIGHT?

DEFENSIVELY, WHAT DO WE IMPROVE?

OVERALL, WHAT WENT WRONG?

DID I DARE GREATLY? HOW?

GAME #17
POST-GAME REVIEW

VERSUS:

WIN or LOSS   FINAL SCORE: _____ _____

HOME or AWAY | DATE/TIME:

OVERALL ASSESSMENT

DID WE DARE GREATLY? YES or NO

HOW DID OUR PERSONNEL PLAY?

OFFENSIVELY, WHAT DO WE IMPROVE?

OVERALL, WHAT WENT RIGHT?

DEFENSIVELY, WHAT DO WE IMPROVE?

OVERALL, WHAT WENT WRONG?

DID I DARE GREATLY? HOW?

GAME #18
POST-GAME REVIEW

VERSUS:

HOME or AWAY   DATE/TIME:

WIN or LOSS   FINAL SCORE: _____ _____

OVERALL ASSESSMENT

DID WE DARE GREATLY?   YES or NO

HOW DID OUR PERSONNEL PLAY?

OFFENSIVELY, WHAT DO WE IMPROVE?

OVERALL, WHAT WENT RIGHT?

DEFENSIVELY, WHAT DO WE IMPROVE?

OVERALL, WHAT WENT WRONG?

DID I DARE GREATLY? HOW?

143

GAME #19
POST-GAME REVIEW

VERSUS:

HOME or AWAY

DATE/TIME:

WIN or LOSS   FINAL SCORE: _____ _____

OVERALL ASSESSMENT

DID WE DARE GREATLY?   YES or NO

HOW DID OUR PERSONNEL PLAY?

OFFENSIVELY, WHAT DO WE IMPROVE?

OVERALL, WHAT WENT RIGHT?

DEFENSIVELY, WHAT DO WE IMPROVE?

OVERALL, WHAT WENT WRONG?

DID I DARE GREATLY? HOW?

GAME #20
POST-GAME REVIEW

VERSUS:

HOME or AWAY | DATE/TIME:

WIN or LOSS   FINAL SCORE: _____ _____

OVERALL ASSESSMENT

DID WE DARE GREATLY? YES or NO

HOW DID OUR PERSONNEL PLAY?

OFFENSIVELY, WHAT DO WE IMPROVE?

OVERALL, WHAT WENT RIGHT?

DEFENSIVELY, WHAT DO WE IMPROVE?

OVERALL, WHAT WENT WRONG?

DID I DARE GREATLY? HOW?

GAME #21
POST-GAME REVIEW

VERSUS:

HOME OR AWAY | DATE/TIME:

WIN OR LOSS   FINAL SCORE: _____ _____

**OVERALL
ASSESSMENT**

**DID WE
DARE GREATLY?** YES OR NO

HOW DID OUR PERSONNEL PLAY?

OFFENSIVELY, WHAT DO WE IMPROVE?

OVERALL, WHAT WENT RIGHT?

DEFENSIVELY, WHAT DO WE IMPROVE?

OVERALL, WHAT WENT WRONG?

DID I DARE GREATLY? HOW?

GAME #22
POST-GAME REVIEW

VERSUS:

HOME or AWAY | DATE/TIME:

WIN or LOSS   FINAL SCORE: _____ _____

OVERALL ASSESSMENT

DID WE DARE GREATLY?   YES or NO

HOW DID OUR PERSONNEL PLAY?

OFFENSIVELY, WHAT DO WE IMPROVE?

OVERALL, WHAT WENT RIGHT?

DEFENSIVELY, WHAT DO WE IMPROVE?

OVERALL, WHAT WENT WRONG?

DID I DARE GREATLY? HOW?

GAME #23
POST-GAME REVIEW

VERSUS:

HOME OR AWAY

DATE/TIME:

WIN OR LOSS   FINAL SCORE: _____ _____

OVERALL ASSESSMENT

DID WE DARE GREATLY?   YES OR NO

HOW DID OUR PERSONNEL PLAY?

OFFENSIVELY, WHAT DO WE IMPROVE?

OVERALL, WHAT WENT RIGHT?

DEFENSIVELY, WHAT DO WE IMPROVE?

OVERALL, WHAT WENT WRONG?

DID I DARE GREATLY? HOW?

GAME #24
POST-GAME REVIEW

VERSUS:

HOME OR AWAY

DATE/TIME:

WIN OR LOSS   FINAL SCORE: _____ _____

OVERALL ASSESSMENT

DID WE DARE GREATLY?   YES OR NO

HOW DID OUR PERSONNEL PLAY?

OFFENSIVELY, WHAT DO WE IMPROVE?

OVERALL, WHAT WENT RIGHT?

DEFENSIVELY, WHAT DO WE IMPROVE?

OVERALL, WHAT WENT WRONG?

DID I DARE GREATLY? HOW?

GAME #25
POST-GAME REVIEW

VERSUS:

HOME OR AWAY   DATE/TIME:

WIN OR LOSS   FINAL SCORE: _____ _____

OVERALL
ASSESSMENT

DID WE
DARE GREATLY?   YES OR NO

HOW DID OUR PERSONNEL PLAY?

OFFENSIVELY, WHAT DO WE IMPROVE?

OVERALL, WHAT WENT RIGHT?

DEFENSIVELY, WHAT DO WE IMPROVE?

OVERALL, WHAT WENT WRONG?

DID I DARE GREATLY? HOW?

GAME #26
POST-GAME REVIEW

VERSUS:

HOME or AWAY

DATE/TIME:

WIN or LOSS   FINAL SCORE: _____ _____

OVERALL ASSESSMENT

DID WE DARE GREATLY?   YES or NO

HOW DID OUR PERSONNEL PLAY?

OFFENSIVELY, WHAT DO WE IMPROVE?

OVERALL, WHAT WENT RIGHT?

DEFENSIVELY, WHAT DO WE IMPROVE?

OVERALL, WHAT WENT WRONG?

DID I DARE GREATLY? HOW?

GAME #27
POST-GAME REVIEW

VERSUS:

HOME or AWAY | DATE/TIME:

WIN or LOSS   FINAL SCORE: _____ _____

OVERALL ASSESSMENT

DID WE DARE GREATLY? YES or NO

HOW DID OUR PERSONNEL PLAY?

OFFENSIVELY, WHAT DO WE IMPROVE?

OVERALL, WHAT WENT RIGHT?

DEFENSIVELY, WHAT DO WE IMPROVE?

OVERALL, WHAT WENT WRONG?

DID I DARE GREATLY? HOW?

GAME #28
POST-GAME REVIEW

VERSUS:

HOME OR AWAY

DATE/TIME:

WIN OR LOSS   FINAL SCORE: _____ _____

OVERALL
ASSESSMENT

DID WE
DARE GREATLY?   YES OR NO

HOW DID OUR PERSONNEL PLAY?

OFFENSIVELY, WHAT DO WE IMPROVE?

OVERALL, WHAT WENT RIGHT?

DEFENSIVELY, WHAT DO WE IMPROVE?

OVERALL, WHAT WENT WRONG?

DID I DARE GREATLY? HOW?

GAME #29
POST-GAME REVIEW

VERSUS:

WIN or LOSS   FINAL SCORE: _____ _____

HOME or AWAY DATE/TIME:

OVERALL
ASSESSMENT

DID WE
DARE GREATLY?   YES or NO

HOW DID OUR PERSONNEL PLAY?

OFFENSIVELY, WHAT DO WE IMPROVE?

OVERALL, WHAT WENT RIGHT?

DEFENSIVELY, WHAT DO WE IMPROVE?

OVERALL, WHAT WENT WRONG?

DID I DARE GREATLY? HOW?

GAME #30
POST-GAME REVIEW

VERSUS:

HOME or AWAY | DATE/TIME:

WIN or LOSS   FINAL SCORE: _____ _____

OVERALL ASSESSMENT

DID WE DARE GREATLY? YES or NO

HOW DID OUR PERSONNEL PLAY?

OFFENSIVELY, WHAT DO WE IMPROVE?

OVERALL, WHAT WENT RIGHT?

DEFENSIVELY, WHAT DO WE IMPROVE?

OVERALL, WHAT WENT WRONG?

DID I DARE GREATLY? HOW?

GAME #31
POST-GAME REVIEW

VERSUS:

HOME OR AWAY | DATE/TIME:

WIN OR LOSS | FINAL SCORE: _____ _____

OVERALL ASSESSMENT

DID WE DARE GREATLY? YES OR NO

HOW DID OUR PERSONNEL PLAY?

OFFENSIVELY, WHAT DO WE IMPROVE?

OVERALL, WHAT WENT RIGHT?

DEFENSIVELY, WHAT DO WE IMPROVE?

OVERALL, WHAT WENT WRONG?

DID I DARE GREATLY? HOW?

GAME #32
POST-GAME REVIEW

VERSUS:

HOME OR AWAY

DATE/TIME:

WIN OR LOSS   FINAL SCORE: _____ _____

OVERALL
ASSESSMENT

DID WE
DARE GREATLY?   YES OR NO

HOW DID OUR PERSONNEL PLAY?

OFFENSIVELY, WHAT DO WE IMPROVE?

OVERALL, WHAT WENT RIGHT?

DEFENSIVELY, WHAT DO WE IMPROVE?

OVERALL, WHAT WENT WRONG?

DID I DARE GREATLY? HOW?

Additional Resources

EXAMPLE FORMS

On the following pages, you can see an example for how each of the forms in this book can be completed. Pay attention to the level of detail that is needed for different sections so that you can most effectively use this book.

Make your answers and responses on this form as personal to you and your goals as possible. The more you use this book, the better you will get at keeping up with these tools throughout the season (and the faster you'll be).

The following forms are located on the pages below:

EXAMPLE FORM
THE 1% APPROACH

GROWTH AREA #1
DESCRIBE GOAL:

Become a clear and accepted leader of the team, on and off the court. Grow ability to use voice during practice, film, and games. Use natural wisdom for game and teamwork in a way that grows the team.

HOW WILL GROWTH BE MEASURED?

Measure growth based on team captains weekly input (Kendrick and Andy). Also get input from Coach Williams.

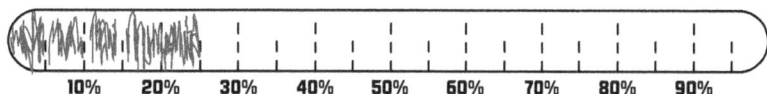

WRITE YOUR GOALS IN DETAIL HERE

TRACK PROGRESS: 10% 20% 30% 40% 50% 60% 70% 80% 90%

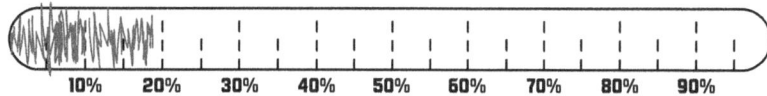

GROWTH AREA #2
DESCRIBE GOAL:

Increase physicality on the court that isn't measured by points scored. This includes rebounds, steals, transitions, traps, etc.

HOW WILL GROWTH BE MEASURED?

Measure based on basic stats. Measure based on personal assessment after each practice and game.

TRACK PROGRESS: 10% 20% 30% 40% 50% 60% 70% 80% 90%

GROWTH AREA #3
DESCRIBE GOAL:

Be the first to arrive and the last to leave practice. Every day.

HOW WILL GROWTH BE MEASURED?

Attendance at practice.

TRACK PROGRESS AS IT OCCURS DURING THE SEASON

TRACK PROGRESS: 10% 20% 30% 40% 50% 60% 70% 80% 90%

EXAMPLE FORM
PROGRAM PLAYS

NAME OF PLAY:
Z-23

TYPE:

(OFFENSIVE)   DEFENSIVE

IN WORDS, DESCRIBE THIS PLAY:
Get set in a 1-3-1. The 1 passes to the 2 and then the 4 shifts to block on ball-side. The 3 moves higher up, the ball goes back to the 1, who passes to 3. Then the 4 moves again, cutting around the 5's screen. The 3 can then: shoot the ball, pass to the 4, or if the defense attacks the 4, pass to the 5 on the inside.

WHEN SHOULD THIS PLAY BE USED?
We should use this when a 2-3 zone defense is being used, which is pretty common. If the team has good bigs, this will allow us to move the ball to an open shot outside, or to make a good pass to our post after we run the play.

WHY IS THIS PLAY EFFECTIVE?
When teams have good or several bigs, they will be protecting the paint. This allows us to move the ball around forcing the team to adjust. Plus, our bigs can screen to help open up a couple of shooting options.

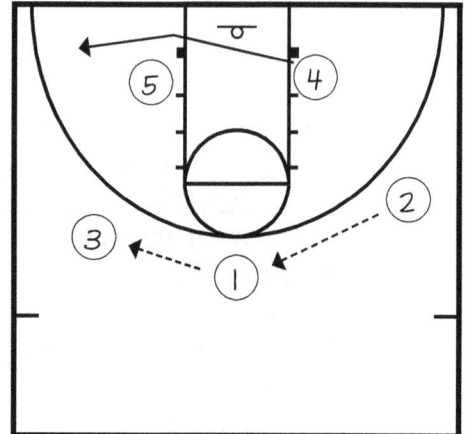

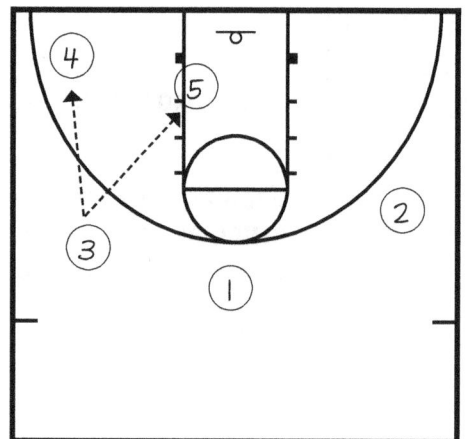

THIS PLAY IS CREDITED TO MICHIGAN STATE UNIVERSITY'S BASKETBALL PROGRAM/ T. IZZO.

WHAT IS MY ROLE IN THIS PLAY?
As a 3, I need to be ready for the ball from the 1. I have options to shoot or to get it to the 4 or the 5 based on whoever is open.

WHAT KIND OF TEAM DO WE USE THIS PLAY AGAINST?
Teams that use a 2-3 zone. Teams that are protecting the paint with their bigs. Teams that are less athletic than us.

WEEK #7:

December 15-21, 2025
DATES

WEEKLY SCHEDULE

MONDAY
Practice 4:45-6:45

TUESDAY
Shootaround 4
Bus 5
Game 7:30 at North

WEDNESDAY
Film 4-5
Practice 5-6:45

THURSDAY
Practice 4:45-6:45

FRIDAY
Shootaround 4:30
Game 7:30 v Lakeside

SATURDAY
Practice 7:30-9:30
Team Breakfast 9:30

SUNDAY
Form shooting at the park

MY 1% TO DO LIST

GOAL #1

Leadership: this week I want to do less talking and more action during practice. Things like staying after to clean up, checking in with teammates before practice to make sure everyone has a ride on the group chat.

GOAL #2

Physicality: we have 2 games this week. I want to lead the team in rebounds for both games.

GOAL #3

Showing Up: I've been doing well each week being the first and last player. I want to keep that up. No one has really noticed this yet, but that's okay. It's important for me.

MY CHECKLISTS

PRACTICE-PREP
GEAR/SHOES: Packing my bag at night each day
NUTRITION: Peanut butter/ banana for practice
RIDES: Kendrick is picking me up each day
TREATMENT: No treatment needed right now
ASSIGNMENTS: Guessing I will have film this week

GAME-PREP
GEAR/SHOES: Doing laundry on Monday for the week
NUTRITION: Mom's making sandwiches for games
RIDES: Kendrick is picking me up
TREATMENT: No treatment needed right now
MENTAL: DND on phone, music playlist is ready

SCHOOL
HOMEWORK: Math will be heavy this week
TESTS/QUIZZES: Quiz in science on Friday
ATTENDANCE: No issues this quarter so far
OTHER: Need to finish credit recovery soon

EXAMPLE FORM
FILM & SCOUTING REPORT

FILM & SCOUTING REPORT

HOME: Lakeside	**DATE:** 12/11
GUEST: North	

ASSIGNED COACH: Williams
ASSIGNED PLAYER: Kendrick

HOME | **GUEST**

SCORE: 1ST 10 2ND 22 3RD 40 4TH 56

SCORE: 1ST 14 2ND 30 3RD 46 4TH 66

MAN: (Y) or N
ZONE SETS: Primarily a 2-3 zone, occasionally 1-2-2

PRESS: (Y) or N
DETAILS: Half-court press primarily

MAN: (Y) or N
ZONE SETS: Primarily a 1-3-1 zone, when used

PRESS: (Y) or N
DETAILS: Full-court press, but not strong

DRAW THE OFFENSIVE SETS YOU SEE HERE →

OFFENSE SETS:
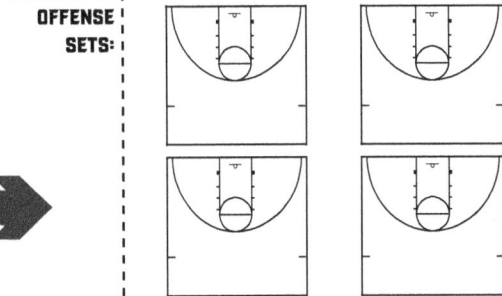

OFFENSE SETS:
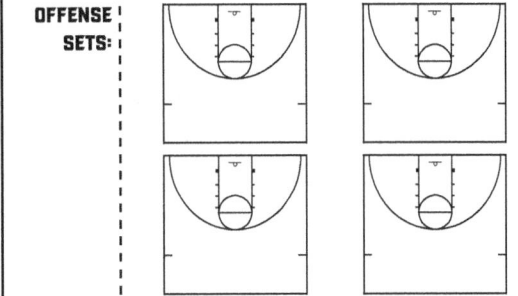

SHOT CHART: Q1 Q2 Q3 Q4
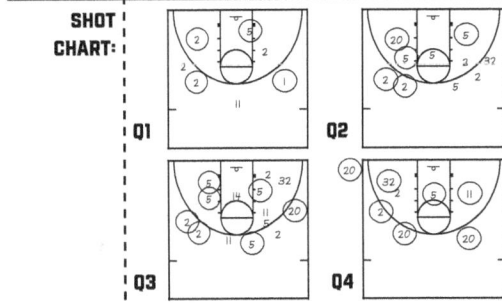

SHOT CHART: Q1 Q2 Q3 Q4
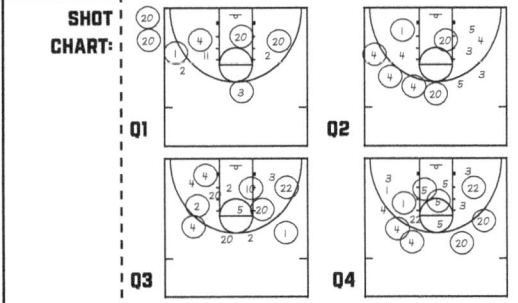

#	REBs	FLs	STs	TOs	#	REBs	FLs	STs	TOs
2	II	III	I	III	14		I		II
5	IIIIIII	IIII	III	I	32	I		I	III
II	III	I		I					
10	I								
I	III	III	I						
20	I	I		II					

#	REBs	FLs	STs	TOs	#	REBs	FLs	STs	TOs
I	I	IIII	IIII	I	22	I			I
3	I	I	II		30	II	I		
5	IIIII	III	I		10	I	II	II	
II	IIII	II		II					
20	IIIIIII	III	III						
4	II		II	III					

164

FOR SCOUTING REPORTS:

WHO ARE THE KEY PERSONNEL TO KNOW OF? WHY?

#4 is a 3 point shooter. High scorer.
#20 will out-rebound us if we aren't aware. Can shoot anywhere.
#5 is a strong defender. Good shooter.

WHAT ARE OUR LIKELY MATCHUPS?

Kendrick on #4
Andy on #20
Martin on #5
Marcus/Martin on #11

**WHICH PLAYS SHOULD WE
USE AGAINST THIS TEAM?**

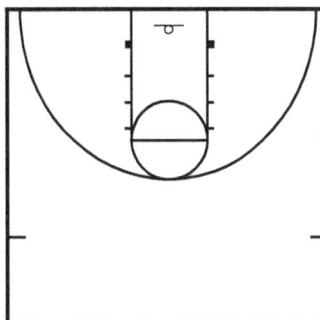

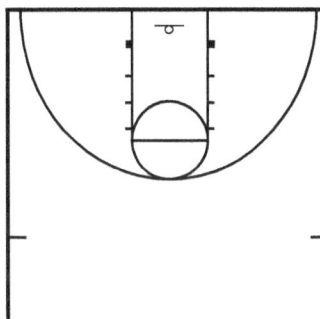

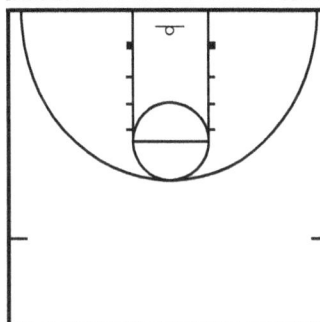

DO THEY LIKE TO RUN?	(YES) OR NO
WHERE DO THEY SHOOT FROM?	LEFT, RIGHT, OR (BOTH)
DO THEY ATTACK THE BASKET?	YES OR (NO)
DO THEY PRESS?	(YES) OR NO
IS MAN DEFENSE:	(TIGHT) OR SAGGING

HOW DO THEY DEFEND THE POST? FORWARDS?
Will try to deny passes. Will contest entry.

Good footwork against forwards. Good at anticipating.

DEFENSIVE WEAK POINTS? PRESS WEAK POINTS?
Primarily man defense, so we can tire them out.

Full-court press is weak. Transitions are crucial.

HOW DO WE COMBAT THEIR OFFENSIVE APPROACH?
Deny 3s at every point possible. #20 is evenly paced throughout game, need to tire him out. Deny momentum of #4. Defensive rebounds are crucial.

HOW DO WE COMBAT THEIR DEFENSIVE APPROACH?
Will win this game in transitions, we can run faster if we never let up. They will trap at half-court.

HOW WILL I DARE GREATLY? HOW WILL I IMPROVE ON MY 1% GOALS?
My goal is to increase rebounds and stops this game. That will require me to dare greatly because I know this is better than me taking every shot.

EXAMPLE FORM
POST-GAME REVIEW

GAME #6
POST-GAME REVIEW

VERSUS: North

(HOME) OR AWAY

DATE/TIME: 12/13 7:30p

(WIN) OR LOSS   **FINAL SCORE:** 78 71

OVERALL ASSESSMENT
We won with our athleticism, but not because we played well.

DID WE DARE GREATLY? YES OR (NO)

HOW DID OUR PERSONNEL PLAY?
Martin and Kendrick played well in terms of shooting. We had good shots to take and we did. I don't think coach is happy with our effort though, and I don't disagree with him.

OFFENSIVELY, WHAT DO WE IMPROVE?
I can't think of anything to improve on from this game offensively, other than our transition speed.

OVERALL, WHAT WENT RIGHT?
We were hot tonight from the 3. We focused on shooting because of that momentum and took advantage of it.

DEFENSIVELY, WHAT DO WE IMPROVE?
We got lazy on defense...we were making shots and felt like we could slack off. That was dumb because this was an easy team to defend. I know we're gonna run for this.

OVERALL, WHAT WENT WRONG?
Because our shots were going in we didn't get back on transition like we normally do. We also didn't press or trap like we knew we could have. We got lazy with our defense because we had the lead but North was starting to come back at the end.

DID I DARE GREATLY? HOW?
I can say that I did dare greatly. I heard a lot of yelling in the crowd and didn't let it affect me. Normally I would try to react back to the crowd, but I ignored them. That was hard, but it's keeping my head in the game.

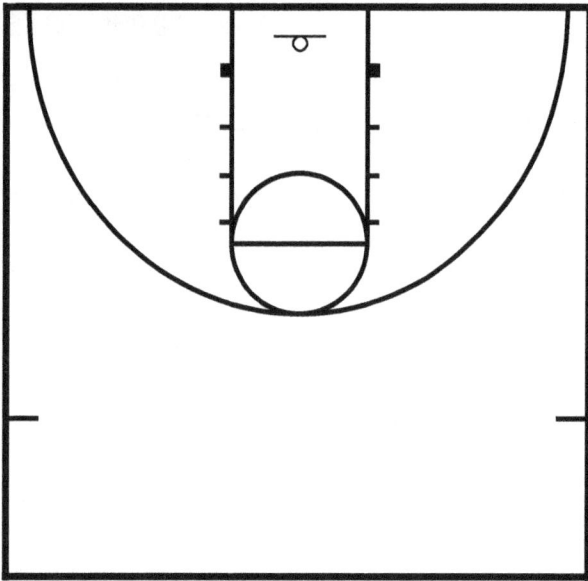
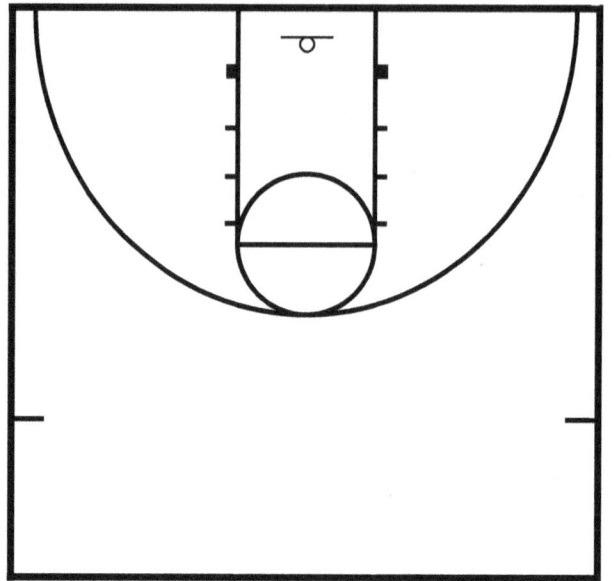
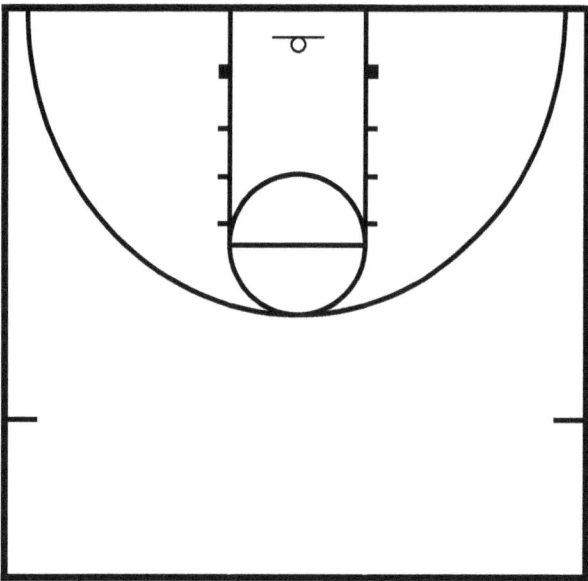
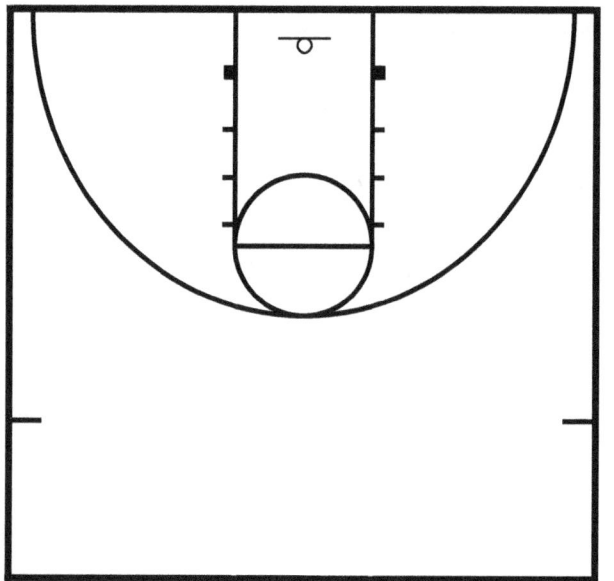
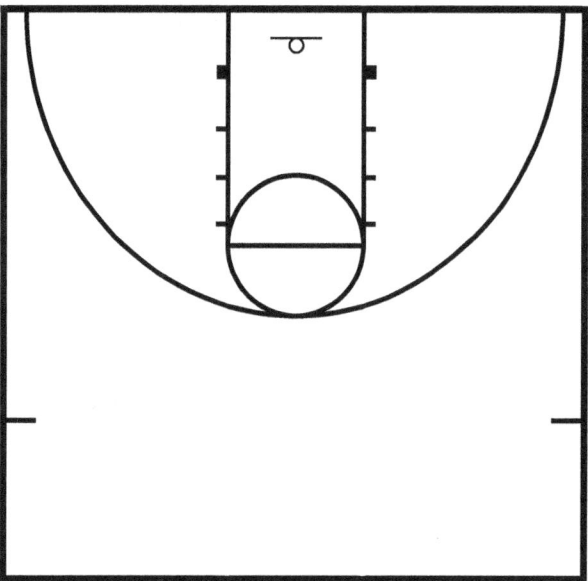
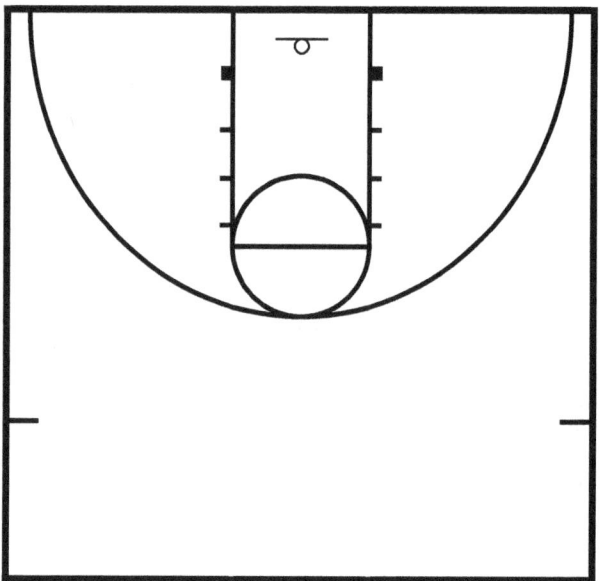

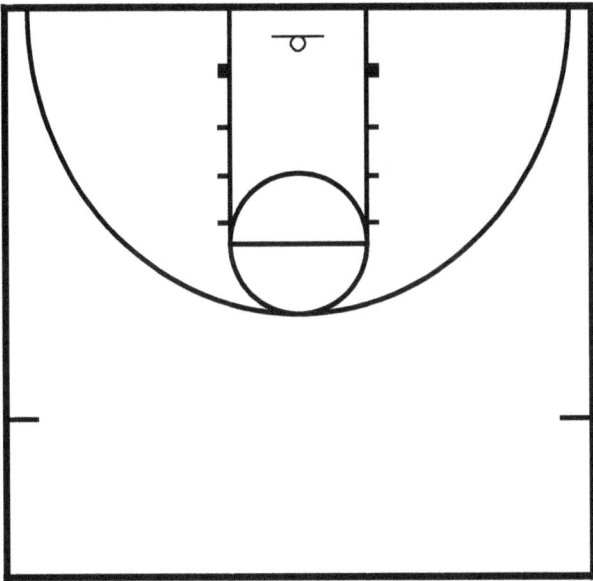
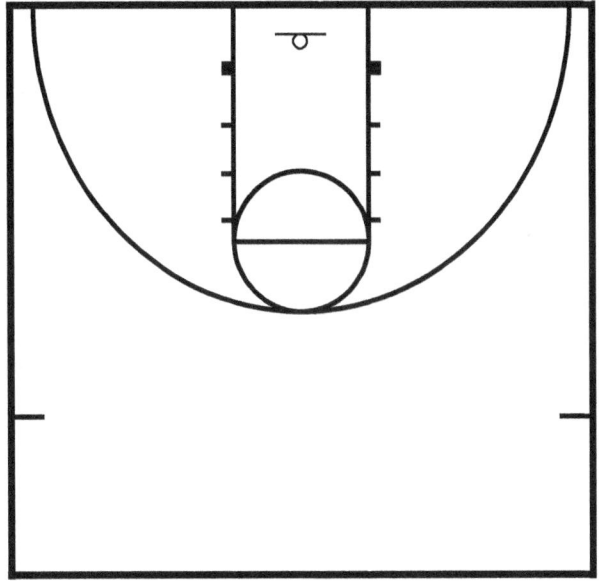
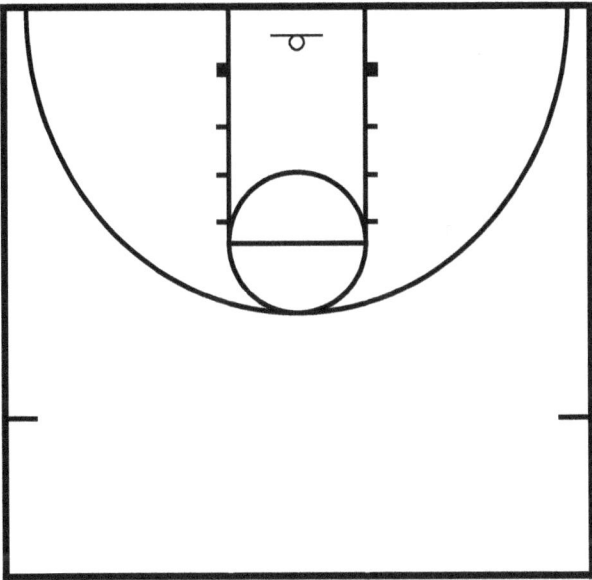
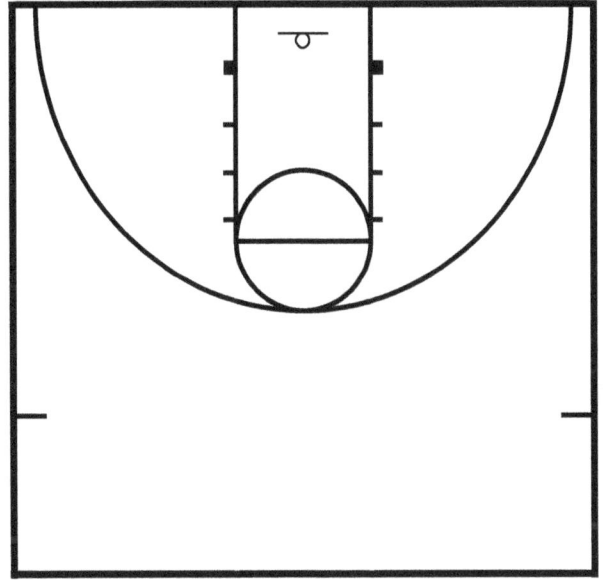
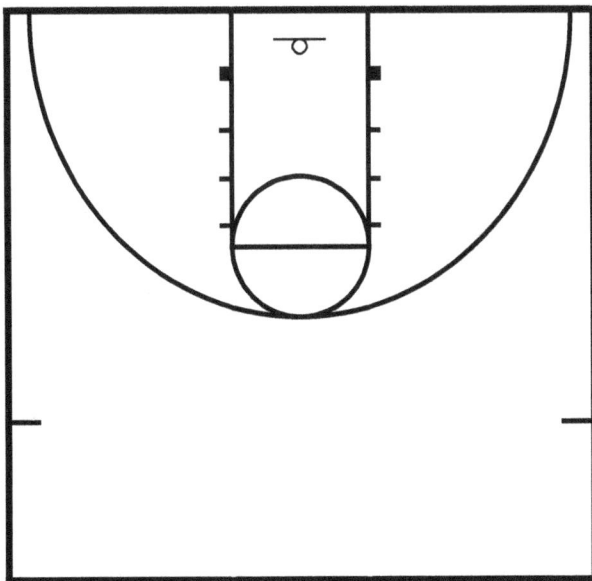
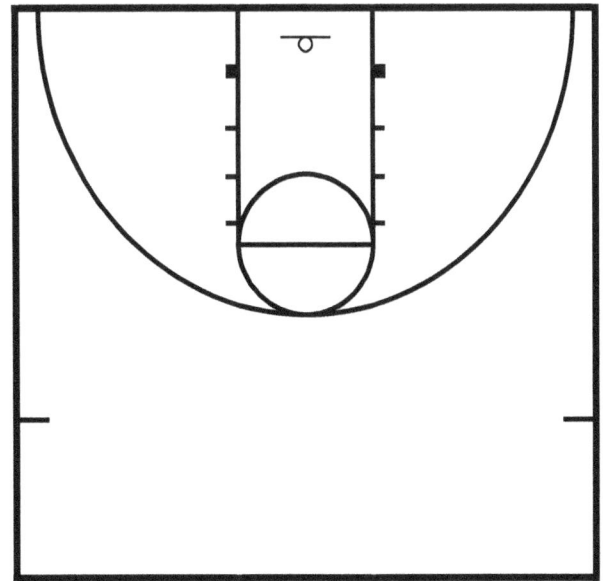

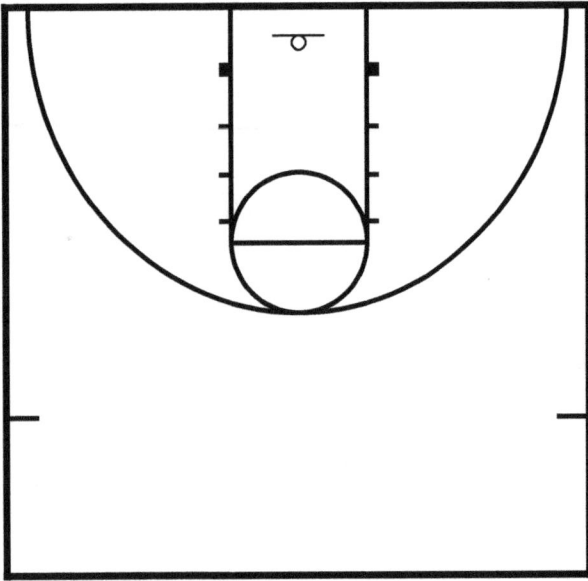
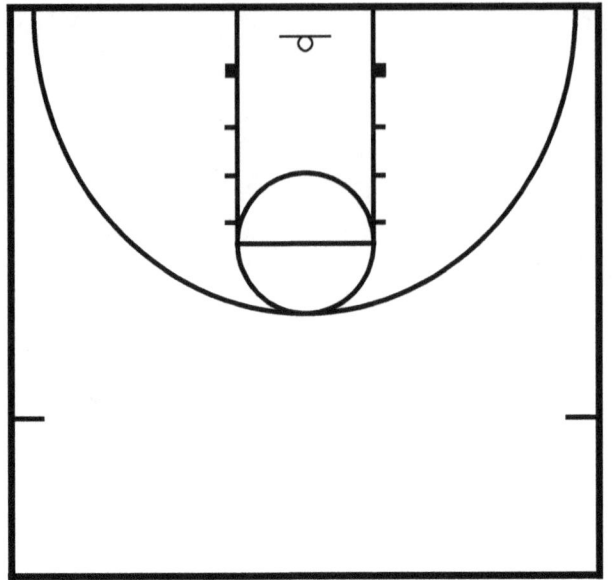
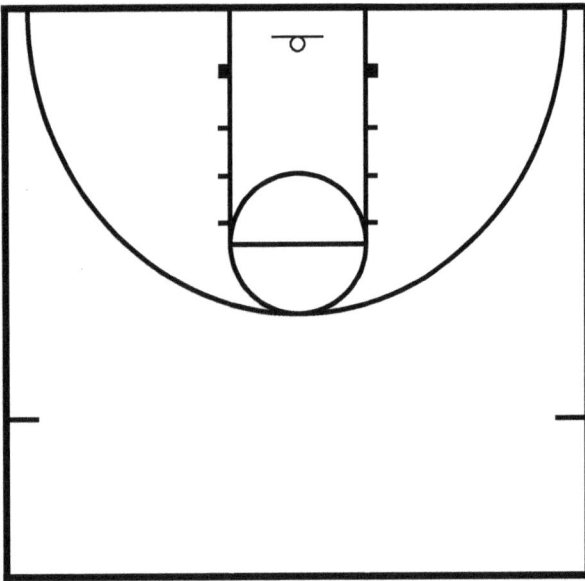
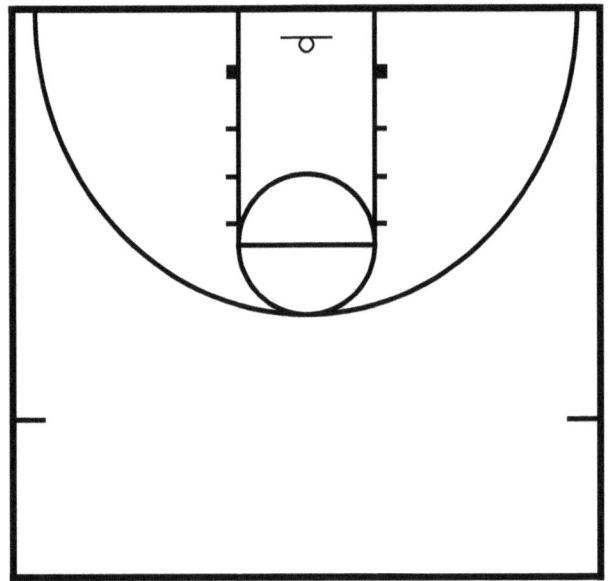
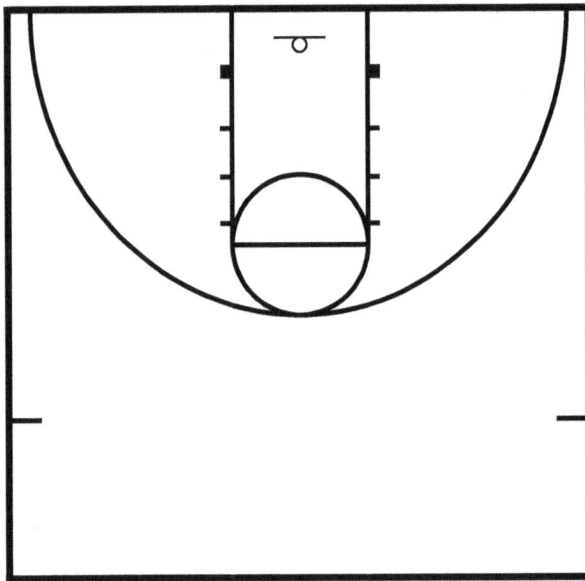
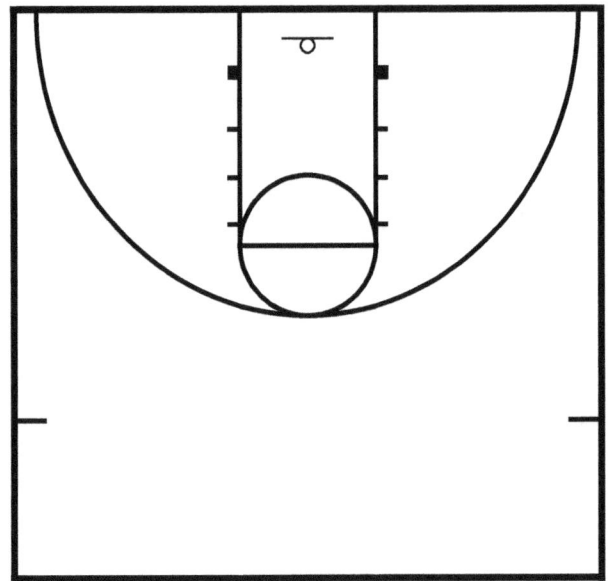

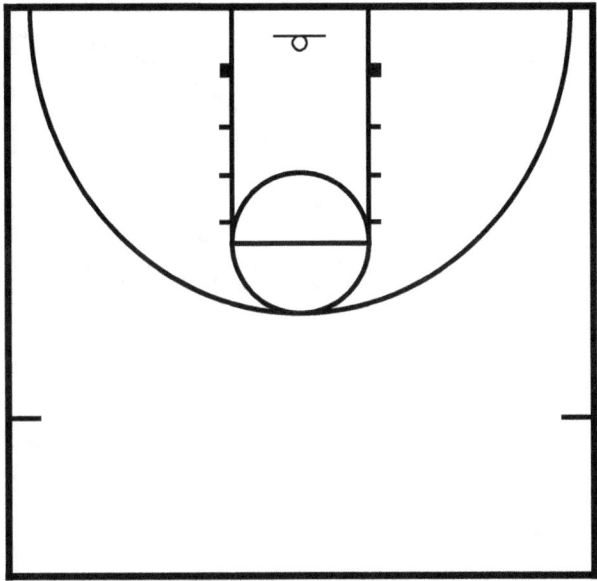
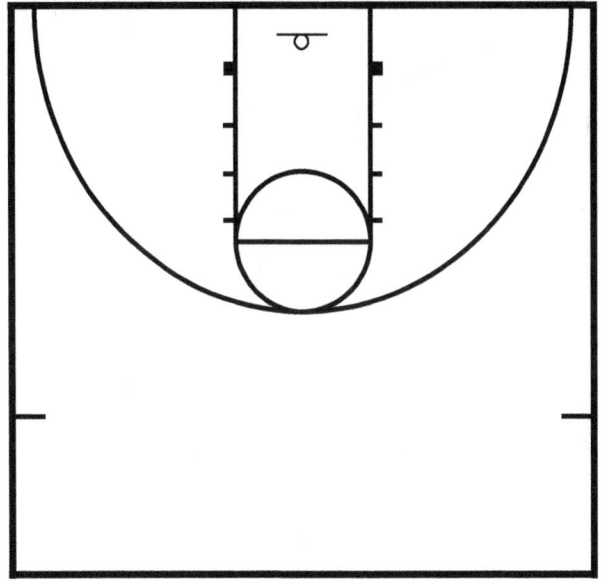
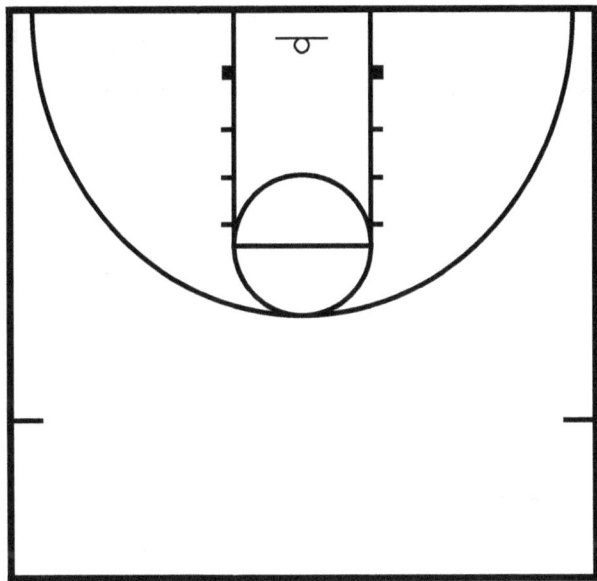
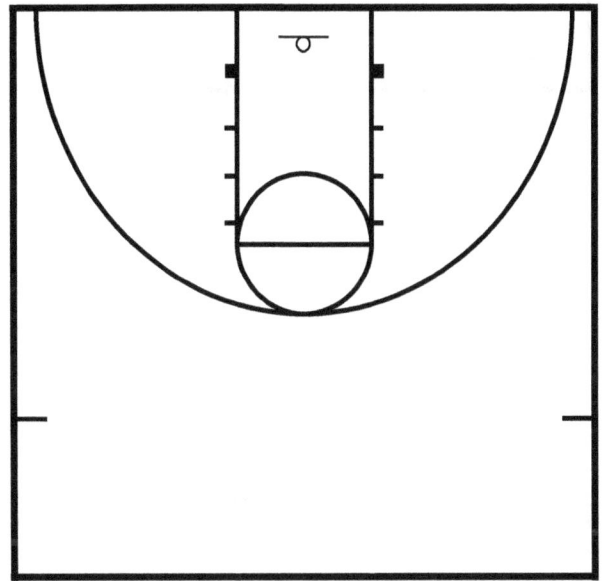
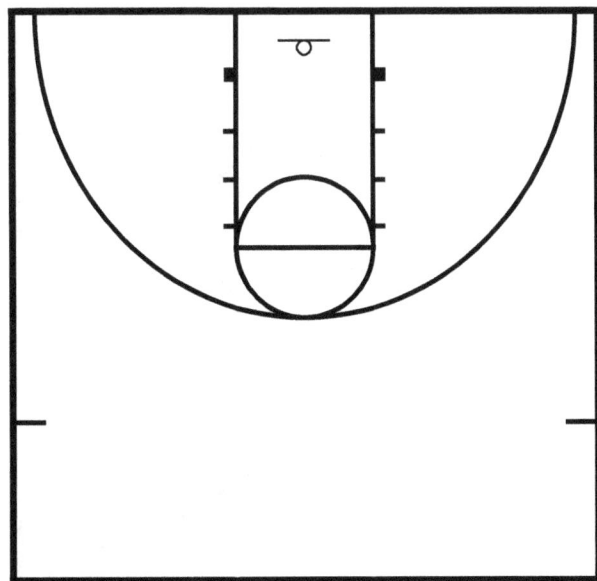
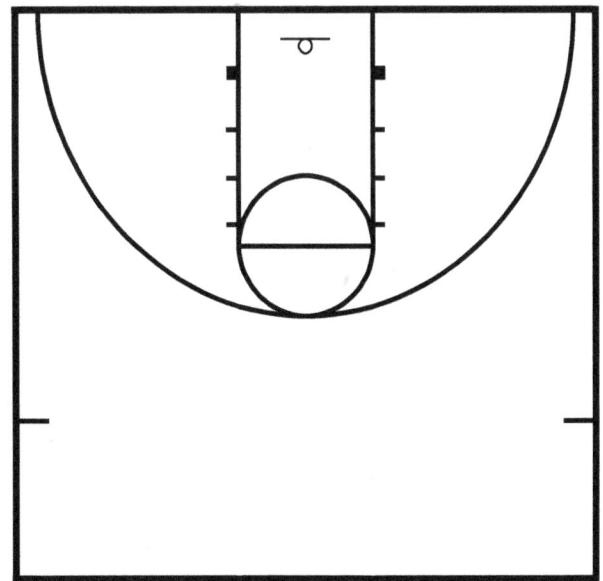

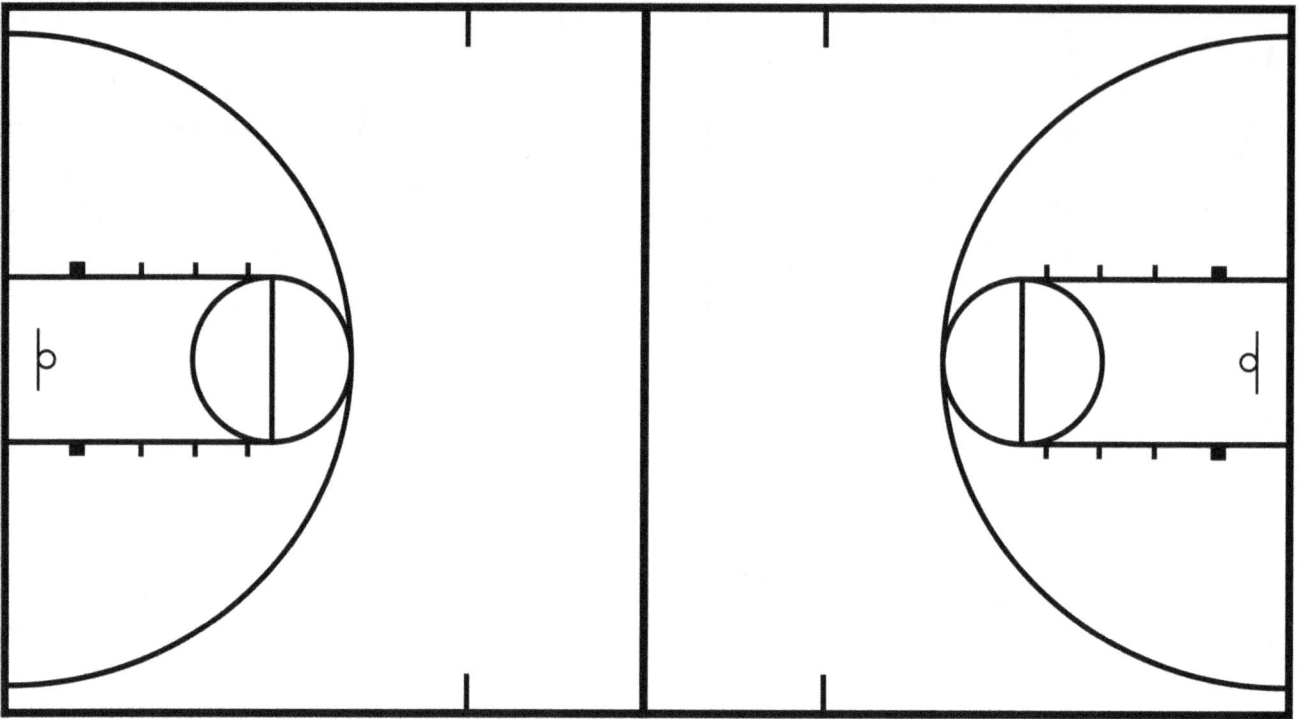

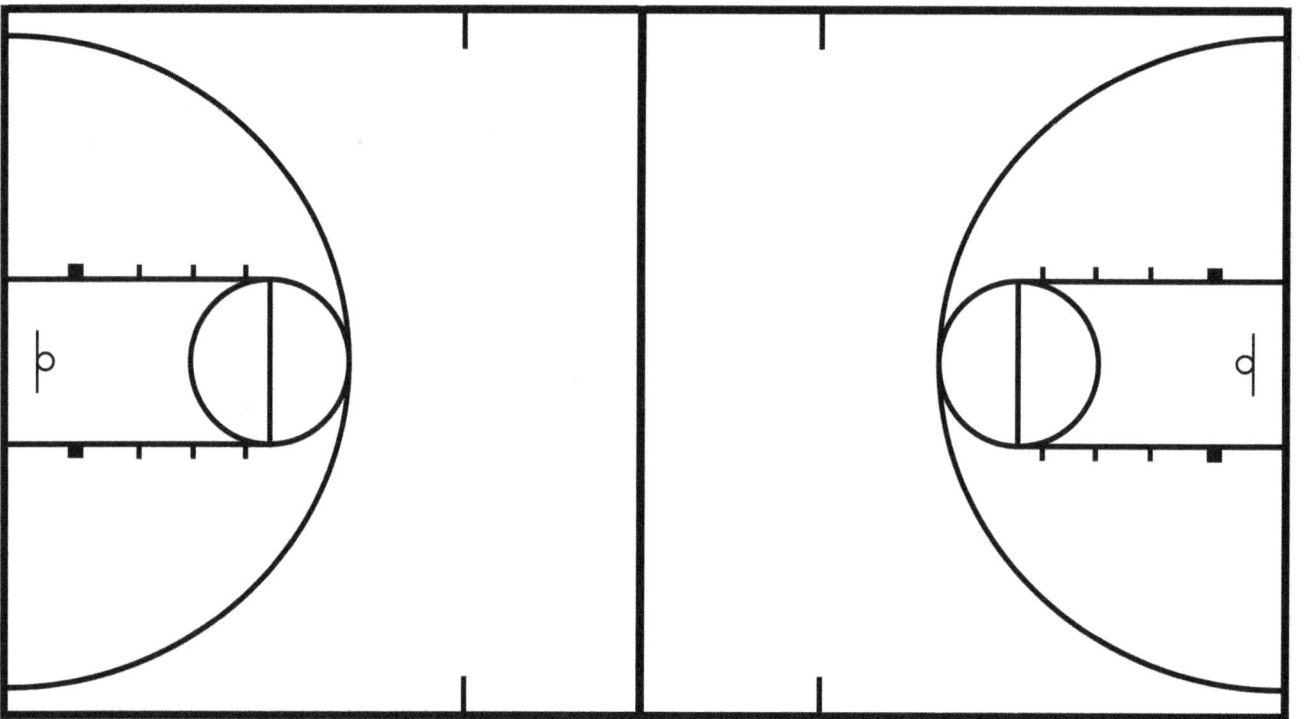

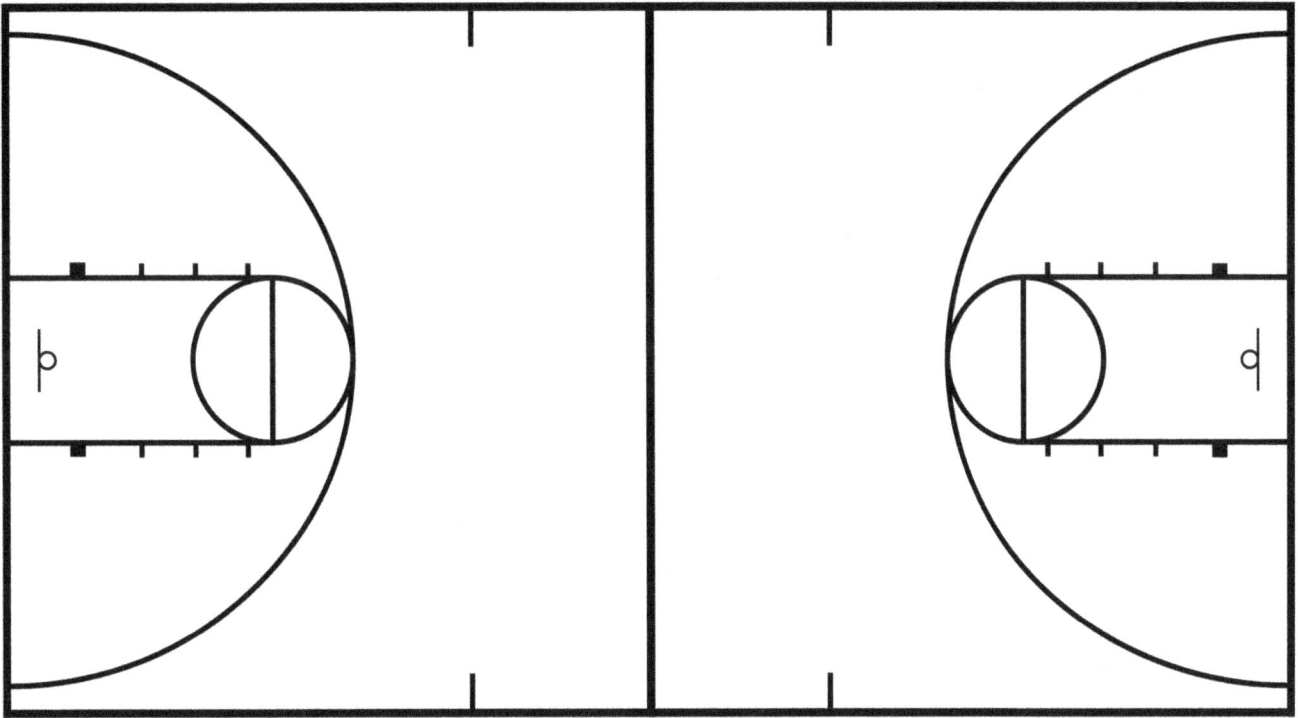

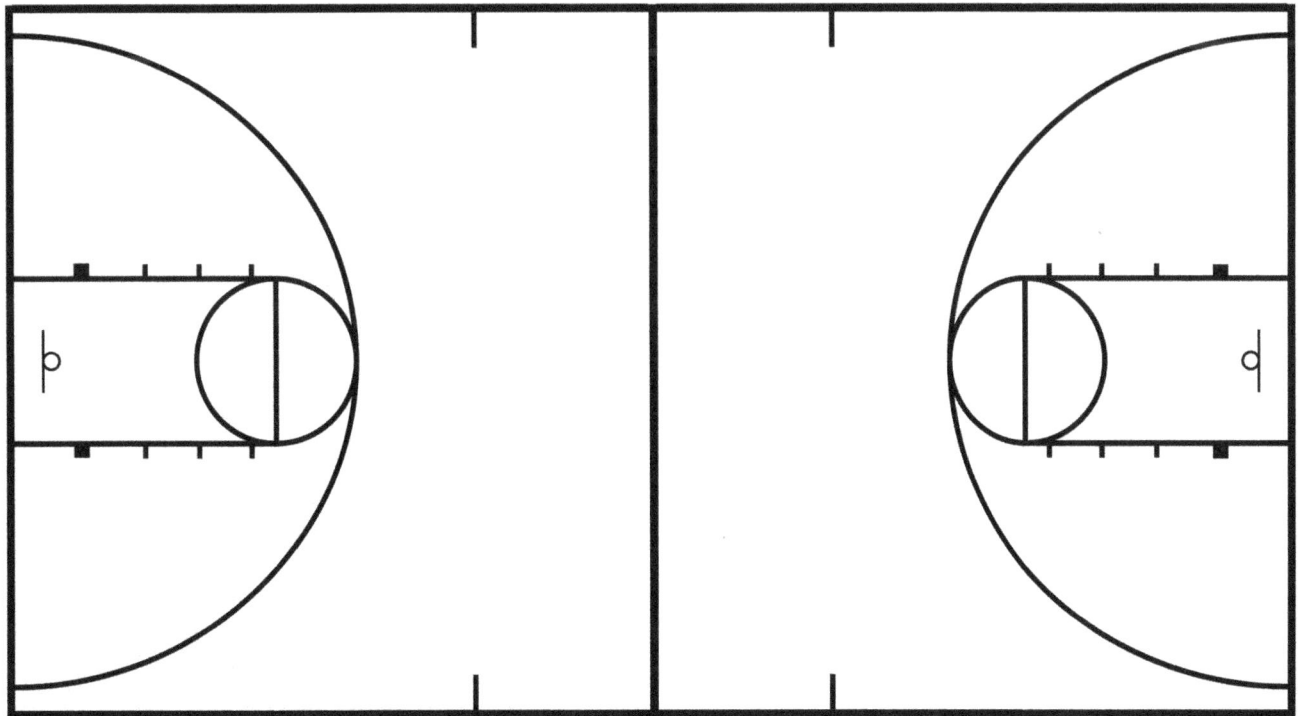

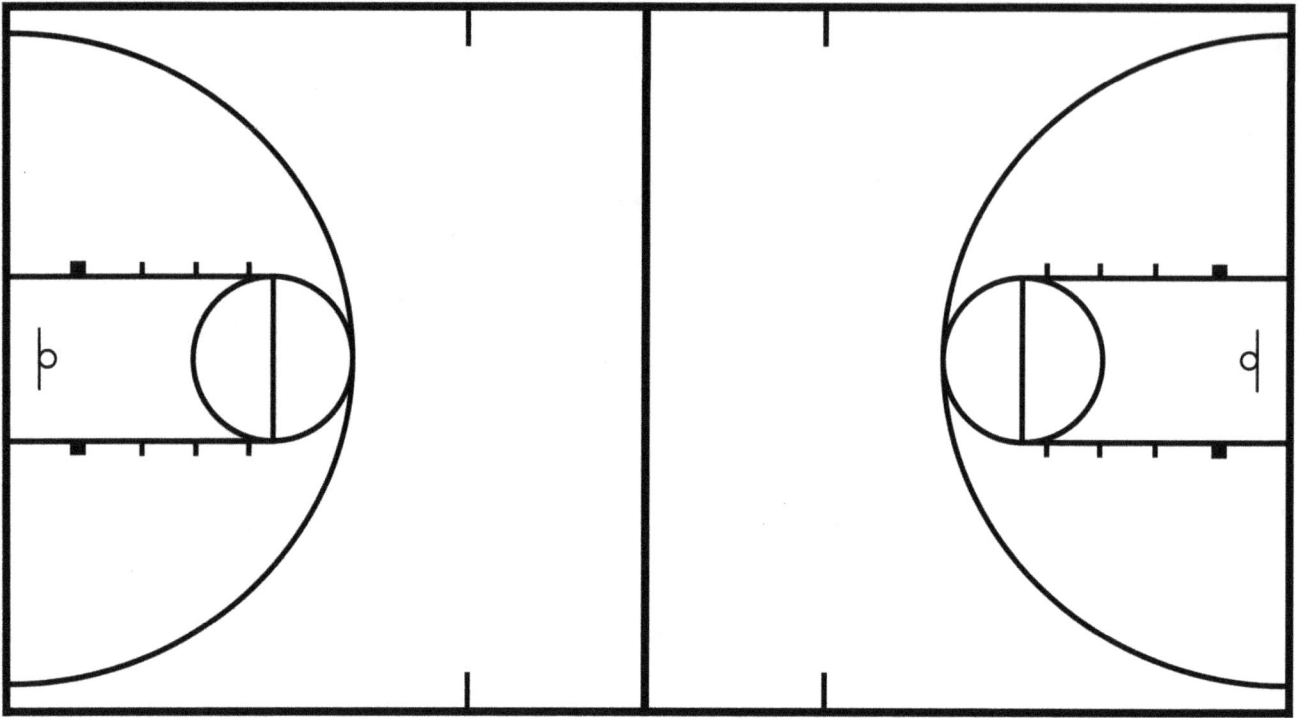

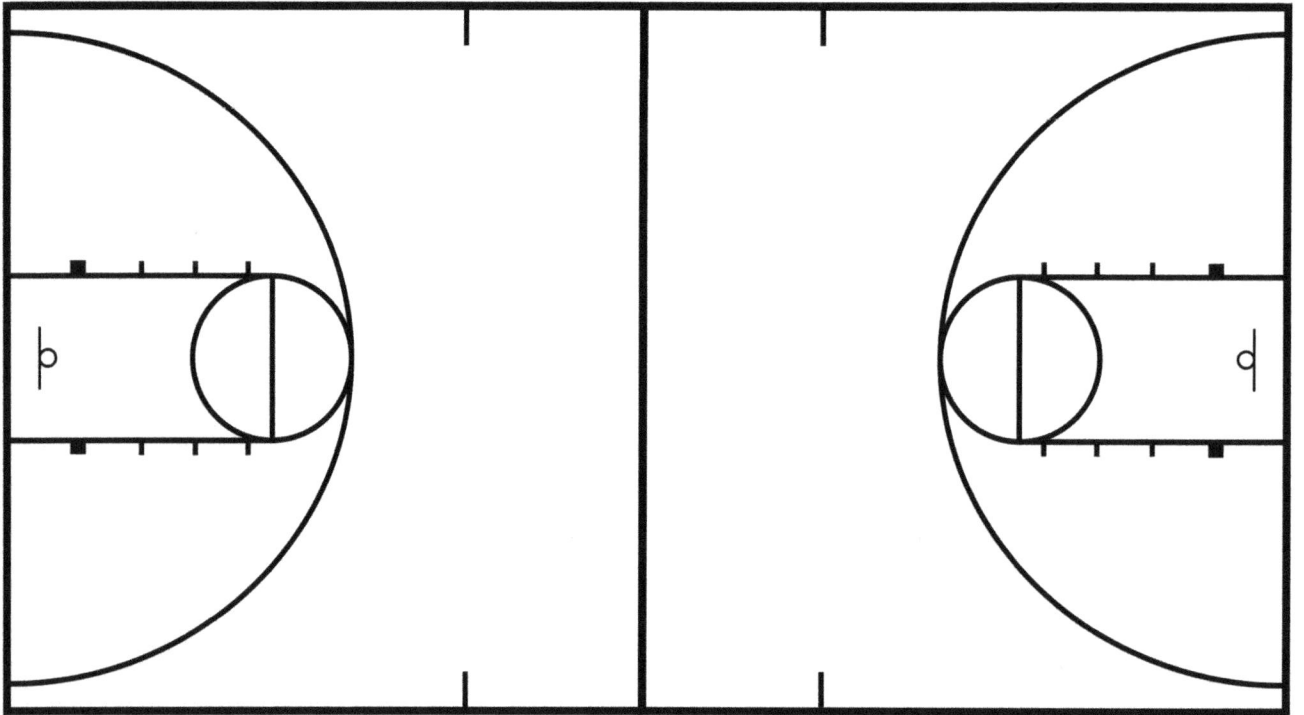

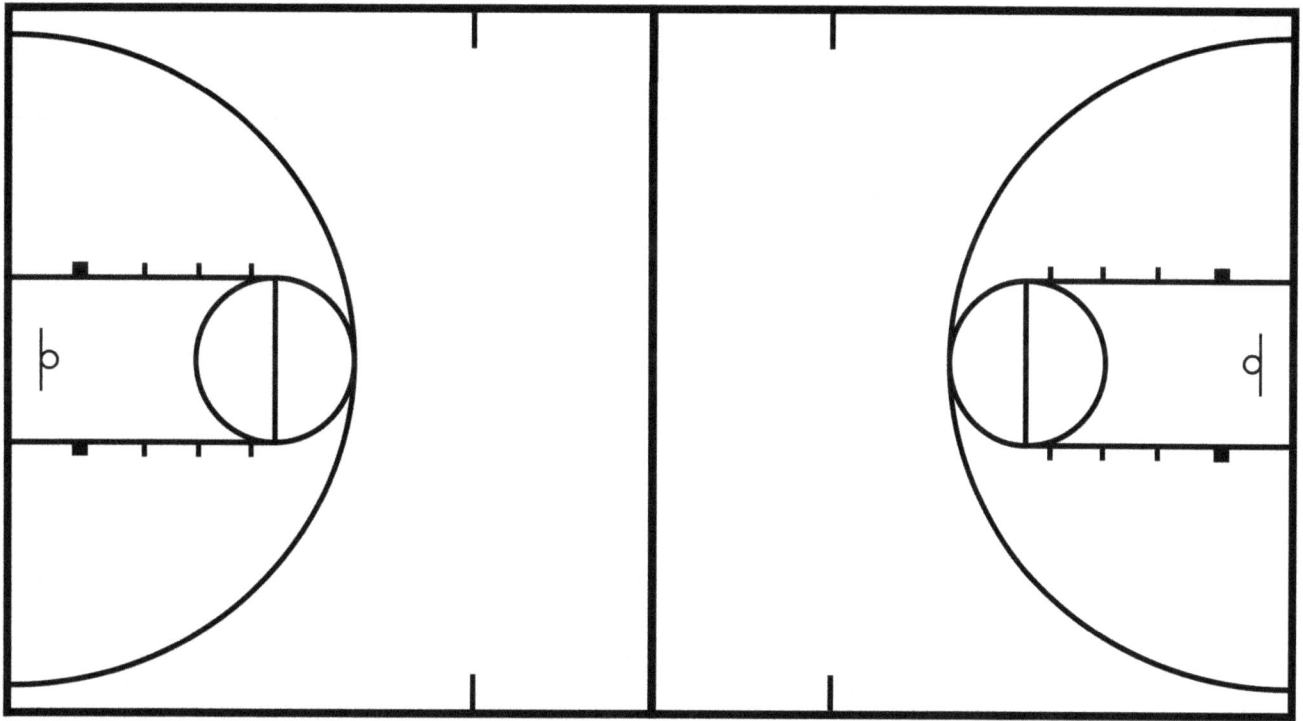

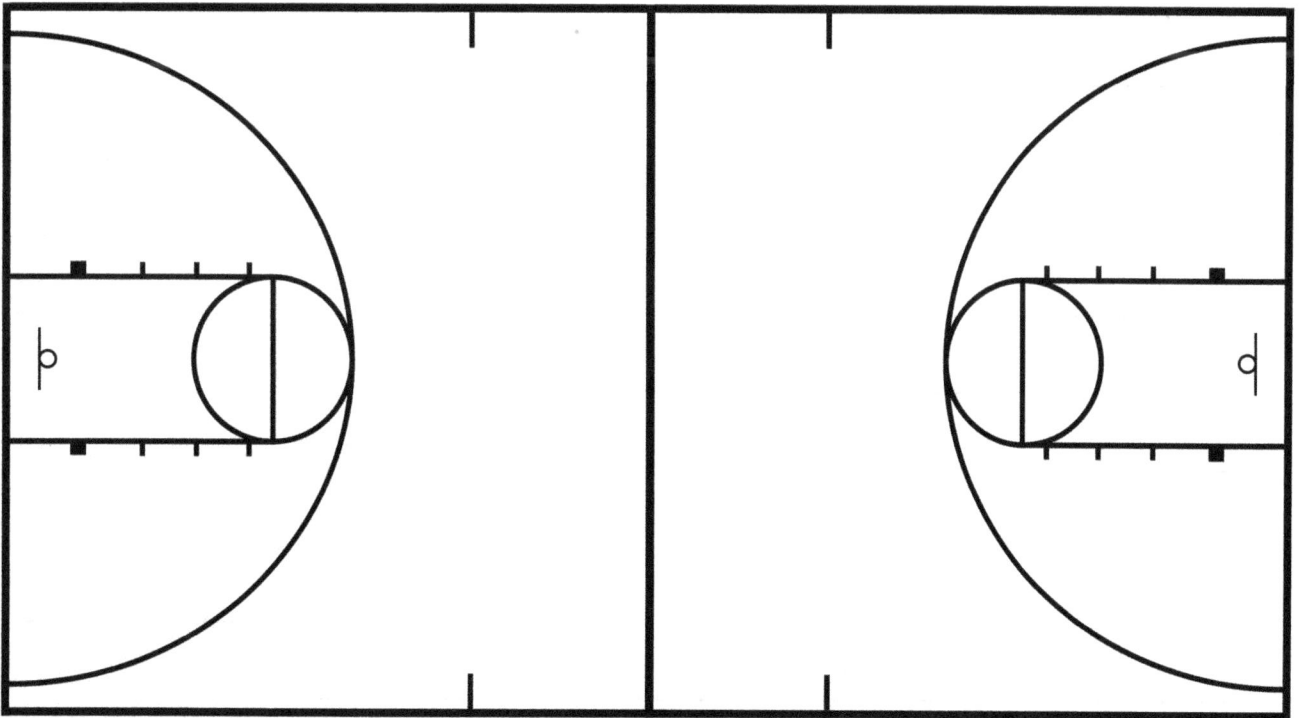

NOTES

NOTES

NOTES

www.ingramcontent.com/pod-product-compliance
Lightning Source LLC
Chambersburg PA
CBHW081149090426
42736CB00017B/3246